中国老翡翠
EARLY MODERN CHINESE JADEITE

十七至二十世纪中国翡翠艺术
Chinese Jadeite Art from the 17ᵗʰ to the 20ᵗʰ Century

上
Volume I

钟富苗　古　方　编著
Zhong Fumiao and Gu Fang

文物出版社
Cultural Relics Press

图书在版编目（ＣＩＰ）数据

中国老翡翠：十七至二十世纪中国翡翠艺术 / 钟富苗, 古方编著. -- 北京：文物出版社, 2020.12
ISBN 978-7-5010-6841-8

Ⅰ.①中… Ⅱ.①钟…②古… Ⅲ.①翡翠－收藏－中国－17-20世纪 Ⅳ.①G262.3

中国版本图书馆CIP数据核字(2020)第210709号

中国老翡翠：十七至二十世纪中国翡翠艺术

编　　者　钟富苗　古方

责任编辑　赵磊　徐旸
责任印制　苏林

出版发行　文物出版社
社　　址　北京市东直门内北小街2号楼
邮政编码　100007
网　　址　www.wenwu.com
邮　　箱　web@wenwu.com
经　　销　新华书店
制版印刷　天津图文方嘉印刷有限公司
开　　本　889×1194mm　1/16
印　　张　50.5
版　　次　2020年12月第1版
印　　次　2020年12月第1次印刷
书　　号　ISBN 978-7-5010-6841-8
定　　价　1898.00元（全三册）

《中国老翡翠——十七至二十世纪中国翡翠艺术》编辑委员会

主　　编　　钟富苗

学术顾问　　古　方

器物鉴定　　古　方

委　　员　　刘　俊　张　瑾　余泳澎　梁前辉

　　　　　　徐　旸　向　东　张崇檀　王丽明

　　　　　　杨绍斌　谢　方　向琪琪

器物说明　　李红娟

文物摄影　　宋　朝　张　冰

（本书所收录器物，均符合其标称历史年代，来源均清晰合法。）

钟富苗
Zhong Fumiao

浙江绍兴人，曾任北京华夏中豪发展有限公司董事长，重庆工发投资发展有限公司总裁，重庆市浙江商会常务副会长，联合国工业发展组织采购基地（筹）主任。现任中和艺术（美国）发展有限公司董事长，瑾瑜文化艺术（重庆）有限公司董事长，瑾瑜山房主人。从事中国文物艺术品收藏研究近三十年，现主要收藏和研究中国近代翡翠艺术品。

Born in Shaoxing City, Zhejiang Province, Zhong once served as President of Beijing Huaxia Zhonghao Development Co., Ltd. and Chongqing Gongfa Investment Development Co., Ltd., Executive Vice Chairman of Zhejiang Chamber of Commerce in Chongqing, and Director of UNIDO International Industrial Commodities Purchasing Base. Now he is President of Zhonghe Arts (the U.S.) Development Co., Ltd. and Jinyu Culture & Arts (Chongqing) Co., Ltd., as well as the owner of The Jinyu Shanfang Collection. For nearly three decades, Zhong's research interest has been focused on collection of Chinese artifacts. More recently, he has paid growing attention to collecting and studying jade artifacts of modern China.

古　方
Gu Fang

北京人，中国文化艺术发展促进会收藏文化专业委员会主任。毕业于北京大学考古系（1986 年）和中国社会科学院研究生院考古系（1989 年）。主要从事中国古代玉器的鉴定和学术研究。主编《中国出土玉器全集》（2005 年）、《中国古玉器图典》（2007 年）、《中国传世玉器全集》（2010 年）和《加拿大皇家安大略博物馆藏中国古代玉器》（2016 年）。

Born in Beijing, Gu is Director of Specialized Committee of Collection and Culture, China Society for the Promotion of Cultural and Art Development. He majored in archaeology and graduated from Peking University in 1986 and Graduate School of Chinese Academy of Social Sciences in 1989. Engaging in authentication and academic research in ancient Chinese jades, Gu compiled *The Complete Collection of Jades Unearthed in China* (2005), *The Pictorial Handbook of Ancient Chinese Jades* (2007), *Chinese Jades in Traditional Collections* (2010), and *Ancient Chinese Jades from the Royal Ontario Museum* (2016).

凡　例

◆　一、《中国老翡翠——十七至二十世纪中国翡翠艺术》（以下简称本书）是以器物图片为主体，系统展示 17–20 世纪中国翡翠工艺品的图书，其中著录器物的时代、名称、材质、尺寸、造型、纹饰及题材寓意等基本要素，其他不作考释。

◆　二、本书分卷原则上以器物类别划分为五类，分上中下三卷。上卷设编委会、目录、图版目录、总序、专论、图版，其余各册只设图版目录、图版。

◆　三、本书选取了 17–20 世纪中国以翡翠为材质加工制作的工艺品，全面系统地反映中国翡翠工艺品的材质、题材、种类、用途和加工工艺，体现了这一门类文物的历史价值、艺术价值和科学价值。

◆　四、本书收录藏品全部来自于瑾瑜山房收藏。其来源于国营文物商店、国内外文物艺术品拍卖行及面向社会征集的流散器物。

◆　五、本书中藏品的定名依照时间、质地、工艺、纹样、器型为主，个别名称参照业界通用名称。

◆　六、本书图版中器物图片凡一器多面展示时，正面、背面、底面、侧面之间以短线示意。局部放大图则加以背景色以示区别。

◆　七、本书中文物的时代采用传统中国朝代名称纪年方法表示。

◆　八、本书中度量衡和数据均采用中华人民共和国法定单位书写。

GUIDE TO READING

1. Ancient Chinese Jadeite: Chinese Jadeite Art from the 17th to the 20th Century (hereafter as Ancient Chinese Jadeite) is a catalog of China's jadeite articles made in the period in question and gives basic information about the items, including the date, name, material, design, size, shape and meaning.

2. The three-volume Ancient Chinese Jadeite puts the articles under five categories. Volume I contains the Name List of Editorial Board, Content, Content of Captioned Photos, Preface, Essays, and Captioned Photos. The other two volumes only have Content of Captioned Photos and Captioned Photos.

3. Ancient Chinese Jadeite introduces the jadeite objects made between the 17th and 20th centuries in China and gives an all-round view of the material, themes, types, uses and processing technology of the jadeite objects. The three-volume set demonstrates the historic, artistic, and scientific values of those objects.

4. The objects in Ancient Chinese Jadeite are all from the Jinyu Shanfang Collection. Have been collected from the state-owned antique and curio stores, Chinese and foreign auction houses, and the public.

5. The objects are named after the date, material, technique, design and shape. Some are named as generally recognized.

6. An object may be displayed from the front, back, bottom and side. The side views are hyphened. An enlarged partial view is put against the colored background.

7. The date is in form of the Chinese dynastic era.

8. The measurements and figures are in form of legal units recognized in the People's Republic of China.

总　序

中国古代玉文化，是中华文明十分值得骄傲的文化属性，也是中华文化中十分重要的组成部分。中华先民把美丽的石头演化出了道德层面的精神比拟，以玉比德，成为道德精神的实物化体现，也让重玉、敬玉、爱玉深深地融入中华文明的基因，历八千余年传承至今而不衰。

翡翠自十七世纪开始在中国出现，至十八世纪进入宫廷，从十九世纪开始，随着当时统治阶级对翡翠的偏爱，从而自上而下风靡全国，几乎与和田玉为主的玉器消费并驾齐驱。这种对于翡翠的喜爱，在十九世纪至二十世纪中叶的短短一百五十年里，成为当时全社会的风尚，在继承玉器传统器型与纹饰的基础上，还根据时代特点衍生出很多特有器型与纹饰，如鸦片烟具、雪茄盒、钟表镶嵌等。在二十世纪中叶之后，随着生活方式的改变，传统形式的翡翠开始逐渐退出了中国人的生活。

明清翡翠艺术品，从题材、器型到纹饰上，经历了由模仿到替代的过程。其加工程序及工具与玉器完全一致，其材料选择经历了"类玉为上"到"以翠为美"的审美转变；其题材与纹饰，既有仿古的宫廷作品，也有民俗的吉祥寓意。可以说，同时期玉器所有的，翡翠都有，玉器所没有的，翡翠也因其材料的特点与社会的需求而得以出现。因此，可以肯定的说，翡翠是中国玉文化中的重要组成部分，是古代玉器史的精彩尾声，是开启中华玉文化承前启后发展创新的重要环节与纽带。

由于历史的原因，翡翠工艺品大量的存留于民间，国有馆藏的老翡翠工艺品相较于民间流散而言，可谓沧海一粟，但一直以来并未引起文博部门的重视。在收藏与展示上，至今也没有专门的展览与展示，几家重要的国有博物馆的古代玉器陈列中，翡翠既不成系列且数量较少。在研究与出版上，至今没有一本较为全面地、专业地展示老翡翠的图书，也没有对翡翠的质地种类与颜色名称有过标准性的研究与界定。面对全国数千万的玉器收藏爱好者，以及数量庞大的传世翡翠实物，老翡翠的研究和整理显得十分必要。面对"让文物活起来"的时代发展需求和社会对于翡翠的喜爱，民间收藏交易的活跃，文物艺术品拍卖市场上的火热，老翡翠的著录与出版显得十分急迫。

瑾瑜山房主人钟君，在经营实业的同时，醉心于中国近代翡翠的收藏凡二十年。其藏品数量之大、品类之全堪称一座老翡翠博物馆，以瑾瑜山房藏翡翠为基础的《中国老翡翠——十七至二十世纪中国翡翠艺术》一书，填补了中国古代玉器研究著录的空白，以全集性的形式全面展示了十七至二十世纪中国翡翠的器型、题材、纹饰与老翡翠特有的质地与特点，同时还表现了翡翠的加工工艺与不同地域下的文化面貌，可以说是系统开启中国老翡翠研究不可或缺的工具书，也是对中国玉文化发展补上了重要的一环，可谓功在当代、利在千秋。

是为序。

原故宫博物院院长、国家文物局局长
2019 年 12 月 12 日

PREFACE

The jade culture in ancient China is a proud cultural badge of the Chinese civilization, a salient constitution of Chinese culture. Ancient Chinese associate beautiful jade with nobility and honor. Viewing jade as a physical embodiment of morality, Chinese people have developed a profound obsession with jade over the past 8,000 years. The love and respect toward jade has been deeply rooted in the Chinese culture.

Jadeite first appeared in China in the 17th Century and was introduced to the royals in the 18th Century. As jadeite gradually won the favor of the ruling class in the beginning of the 19th Century, it was soon democratized across the nation. Jadeite almost exceeded nephrite and became the most popular jade among the masses. During the 150 years from the 19th Century to the mid-20th Century, the whole society contracted a fervent passion for jadeite. Apart from traditional jade wares that featured traditional patterns and designs, new jade products characterized with new patterns and styles, such as opium-smoking sets, cigar cases and clock embellishment, were also produced. Following the mid-20th Century, with the change in our lifestyles, jadeite slowly faded out of the Chinese society.

Jadeite artifacts in the Ming and Qing Dynasties experienced a series of changes in terms of their subjects, styles and patterns. Although the processing techniques and the tools used were exactly the same as those for ordinary jade wares, people's aesthetics in jade selection changed as they came to prefer beautiful jadeite t to premium jade. In terms of subjects and patterns, jadeite artifacts could be either vintage-inspired to serve royal families or designed for civilians in expressing good wishes. We could actually say that jadeite artifacts not only inherited all features of ordinary jade wares at that time but also presented new styles and characters requested by the society. Therefore, we can ascertain that jadeite is an important part of the Chinese jade culture, a fascinating epilogue of the ancient jade ware history, and an essential phase in the Chinese jade culture that links classics and modernity, a key step for further development and innovations.

For some historical reasons, a large number of jadeite artifacts are lost among the masses. Those exhibited in museums, owned by the state, only take up a trifling part of the whole collection. Nevertheless, over the past few years, this issue has not drawn much attention of the Department of Relics and Museology. There has not been a single museum up to this date dedicated to jadeite artifacts, and in those national museums, only very few ancient jade wares are on display, and they are not carefully organized or catalogued. Speaking of research and publication, no book has given a thorough, comprehensive and professional discussion of old jadeite. No scientific research has been conducted to clearly define the qualities and colors of different kinds of jadeite. With such an impressive quantity of materials on ancient jade wares compiled and organized by the system, it is, hence, necessary to thoroughly study old jadeite for the need of thousands of jade ware collectors. To "revive cultural relics", a request from the society, considering people's general love toward jadeite, in view of incessant private transactions among collectors, and on account of numerous sales on various auctions, the publishing of a book discussing old jadeite becomes a pressing matter.

The owner Jinyu Shanfang Collection Mr. Zhong, while operating his business, also accumulated a large collection of Chinese jadeites over the past 20 years. His collection is so massive and inclusive that his house is, veritably, an antique jadeite museum. The publishing of the book, "Early Modern Chinese Jadeite: Chinese Jadeite Art from the 17th to the 20th Century", which is based on Mr. Zhong's collection at the Jinyu Mountain House, fills the blank in ancient Chinese jade ware research. The book has an in-depth discussion of the designs, subjects and patterns of Chinese jadeite between the 17th and the 20th Centuries, as well as various qualities and characters of old jadeite. In the meantime, the book also explores the processing techniques and jade cultures in various regions. In a way, this is an essential reference book for old Chinese jadeite research, and a necessary study for the development of Chinese jade culture, which would benefit not only the current society but also later generations.

That is all for the preface.

Lu Jimin
Former Director of the Palace Museum and
Director of the National Cultural Heritage Administration
December 12, 2019

目　录

本卷图版目录

陈设摆件

最爱玉中一抹绿

钟富苗

翡翠本是鸟的名字，惯于生活在河岸水边。"莎草江汀漫晚潮，翠华香扑水光遥"，唐朝诗人唐彦谦在这首题为《翡翠》的诗中，刻画的正是这种体型小巧、美丽惊艳的翠鸟，红色称翡，绿色称翠。

如今，只要大家一说到翡翠，首先想到的是玉石而不是翠鸟。翡翠，是世界上惟一一种以鸟类命名的玉石。至于这一命名的起源，有多种说法，怕是很难考查了。

玉文化是中华文化精神的重要组成部分，玉器在中华文明的形成中起到了巨大的作用。在中华文明萌发的早期，玉用于沟通神灵、祖灵，祭祀天地山川。及至春秋，儒家倡导君子比德于玉，对玉的特性赋予了人格化推崇，从此以后深入人心。从神玉时代，到王玉时代，再到民玉时代，玉器从最早的祭祀天地众神，到后来为王权服务，成为礼制化的象征，再到唐宋以后逐步进入民间，成为中华儿女手中的宝，更是心中的魂。

几千年来形成的根深叶茂的中华玉文化，熏陶了一代又一代的中华儿女。我也是深受玉文化影响的人。

我出生在绍兴会稽山南麓的小舜江畔，从小生活在大家族合居的老台门里。二十世纪七十年代的中国乡村，依然留存着古老的信仰和风俗。同样，对于玉器，我祖父母一辈的老人们满含珍惜之意，老人们手上或多或少都藏着一点翡翠玉器、银元铜钱等老物件，视若传家之宝。

我小时候就受了老辈人的影响，耳濡目染，十几岁时就开始有意识地收藏古玉器、邮票等老物件，至今都还保留着。一有闲暇，就去各处旧物市场搜寻古董玉器等老物件。我比较注重玉器的材质，因此，我早期的玉器收藏以明清玉为主，爱玉比德，我也取屈原《楚辞·九章·怀沙》中"怀瑾握瑜兮，穷不知所示"的美好寓意，给自己的斋号取名为"瑾瑜山房"。

2001 年，正是国家西部大开发战略出台之初，我响应西部大开发的号召，从天堂杭州来到西南重庆投资创业。其时，我在重庆及西南的旧货市场时常能见到老翡翠。也许是小时候的记忆被激活了，我开始专门收藏老翡翠，从此一发不可收拾。

我先是将搜寻的范围从重庆扩展到了西南地区，尤其是川南、云南，那里是中国最早使用翡翠的区域，继而在全国各地古玩市场和收藏家那里寻找老翡翠。2010 年以后，国内市场上能见到的令我满意的老翡翠越来越少了，我又开始去日本、美国、欧洲等海外各国的古董商、收藏家那里寻购，并在苏富比、佳士得等各大拍卖公司竞投老翡翠。近二十年来，我收藏的老翡翠在数量上已有万余件，基本上收全了老翡翠的各个器型，年代范围涵盖了明代早期至民国及创汇期。

随着藏品渐丰，我对老翡翠的产地、历史和流传路径也产生了强烈的穷其根源的想法。这些年来，我深入考察了翡翠的主要产地缅甸，多次走访云南的腾冲、保山、大理、昭通和四川宜宾、江津等地，拜访当地行家、藏家、玉雕工艺大师和行业协会，收集相关文献资料，走遍了老翡翠之路，对于老翡翠的起源和流传史有了一个总体的认识。

据文献记载，翡翠在元代就已经发现了，明代时已经大量制作成器，以民俗风格的佩饰为主，当时主要在西南地区云贵川三省流通。及至清代，翡翠开始为皇家所用，器型得以极大地丰富，制作工艺也有了质的跃升。来自民间的翡翠，终于凤凰涅槃，成为人所皆知的"帝王玉"。

毫无疑问，翡翠玉器是中华玉文化在近代生发出的崭新一脉，为中华玉文化的发展注入了新鲜血液。

《说文解字》释：玉，石之美者。中国人用玉，在很长的历史时期里都是就地取材，玉石不分的。在八千年中华玉文化史中，昆仑玉、独山玉、蓝田玉、岫岩玉等软玉，以及玛瑙、水晶、绿松石、石英石等，都是我们先民的用玉范围。

近代大家章鸿钊先生在《石雅》中曾言：古人辨玉，首德而次符。"德"是玉石的质地，"符"是玉石的色泽。古人用玉虽杂，并非不注重玉石的质地，而是"德"、"符"难以两全。就翡翠而论，北方人识翠，先色后种；而在西南地区，特别是在滇（云南），有滇人重"德"不重"符"之说，识玉论种有浑浊清透之别，取色则有浓阳偏正之分。大理洱海流域地区俗称是一个"偏色王国"，在这里翠玉使用佩戴早于清代，广于民间普通百姓家，家家婆妻嫁女都须得准备高种飘花手镯和高绿的的绮罗玉耳片，所以这里流散沉淀了大量的高种飘花手镯，有最著名的玻璃种飘海草花手镯——段家玉；而"德""符"双重即种色俱佳，最终成为翠玉鉴赏的最高水准和南北共识，如著名的宝石级翡翠——王家玉（帝王绿），这就是断玉的人常说的水天一色。限于当时的交通条件，逾万里之遥穿越博南山，跨过霁虹桥去寻找上好的玉石，委实是一件艰险之事。

材质的不断优化，是中华玉文化进化发展的一条重要脉络。纵观中国玉器史，从新时期时代晚期至春秋战国时代，都是以地方玉石为主，和阗玉极为鲜见。从两汉开始，由于打通了西域交通，和阗玉开始源源不断地流入中土，成为中国玉器的主要用材。至明清时期，翡翠异军突起，并从民间用玉华丽转身为皇家用玉。

历史地看，翡翠后来居上，是玉中新贵，更是被西方公认为宝石。

早期老翡翠的选料，可以说是以白玉为标准，白底青是最流行的。乾隆皇帝最喜欢瓷地阳绿。讲究种水，是到了慈禧以后才有的风尚。

"翠竹法身碧波潭，滴露玲珑透彩光。脱胎玉质独壹品，时遇诸君高洁缘。"这首题为《璟玉高洁缘》的诗，其作者正是乾隆皇帝。乾隆十分喜爱翡翠。据统计，乾隆一生所作诗篇中，已知咏诵翡翠的就有50多首。

老翡翠器型丰富，纹饰多样，琢制工艺十分全面，既可见传统的民俗吉祥文化，也可见皇家宫廷气派。与此同时，老翡翠融合了玉文化与珠宝文化，是中华玉文化具有世界性意义的代表。

改革开放以来，国内玉器研究相关书籍得以大量出版，然而，关于老翡翠的研究专著却鲜见踪影。国内著名古代玉器研究专家古方先生表示，在他的中国古代玉器系列研究论著里，唯独缺少翡翠这一玉文化的重要分支。得悉我的老翡翠收藏基本涵盖了翡翠进入中国以来的所有时间段，从材质到题材，从数量到品级，都构成了一部完整的中国翡翠艺术发展史。在古方先生和文物出版社的鼓励下，希望由我牵头提供藏品，编纂一本能够完整呈现中国老翡翠的全集性图录，经过多次沟通，最后达成了和文物出版社合作出版此书的想法。

老翡翠在中国玉器史中有着显见的重要地位，整理并传承、弘扬中国玉文化的重要分支——翡翠文化，与广大翡翠爱好者分享我们的认知，这正是我们编辑出版这部《中国老翡翠》的缘由。

The Prettiest Shade of green among Jade

Zhong Fumiao

Jadeite (Fei Cui) was originally the name of a bird, which normally inhabits along rivers and waters. The poem "Fei Cui", written by Tang Yanqian in the Tang Dynasty, describes exactly this dainty bird, in which the author wrote, "Evening tides rose along the grassy river bank. The green little bird fluttered across the distant water from the land." For this type of bird, the red one is called Fei and green Cui.

Nowadays, when it comes to the word Fei Cui, people would normally associate it with jade first instead of the bird. Jade is indeed the only stone named after a bird in the world. There are divergent opinions as to the name's origin, which is, perhaps, rather hard to trace at now.

The jade culture is a vital part of the Chinese culture. Jade wares played a pivotal role in the formation of the Chinese civilization. In the early stage of Chinese society, jade was used as a conduit and sacrifice to communicate with gods and ancestors in rituals dedicated to Heaven and Earth. By the Spring and Autumn period, Confucianists had associated jade with morality and nobility and viewed it as the ideal image of an honorable man. Since then, the jade culture has been incorporated into our society. Jade was first used as a sacrifice to gods, then a luxury exclusively for the royals and symbol of feudalism, and then a democratized item after the Tang and Song Dynasties. Jade thus becomes a treasure among Chinese people, a spirit that represents Chinese culture.

The Chinese jade culture, deeply rooted in generations of Chinese people over the past thousands of years, exerts a profound influence on our society.

I was born in Xiaoshun, Shaoxing at the foot of Mount Kueichi, brought up in an ancient Chinese residence while living with the entire family. In the 1970s, old traditions and customs still prevailed in the countryside in China. Therefore, old generations like my grandparents treasured jade wares. Many seniors, more or less, possessed some jade wares and silver coins. They were treated as family treasures.

Influenced by the seniors in the family, I started to collect ancient jade wares and old stamps when I was a teenager. Even today, I still have them. After I graduated from college and started working, I visited thrifty stores in my spare time to search for antiques such as jade. As I paid particular attention to the quality of jade, the jade wares I collected in early years were mainly those from the Ming and Qing Dynasties. Jade is often associated with morality and honor. In Qu Yuan's poem "Huaisha, Nine Pieces, Songs of Chu", the author wrote, "Honorable as I am (Huai Jin Wo Yu Xi), nobody, however, appreciates my jade-like qualities." As such, I named my study "Jin Yu Shan Fang".

In 2001 shortly after the start of the implementation of policies regarding the development of China's Vast Western Regions, I moved from Hangzhou, a city of paradise, to Chongqing in the southwest to start my investment business. At that time, I often came across old jadeite in the flea market there. The old memories of my childhood suddenly came flowing into my mind. I started to collect old jadeite and thus embarked on my journey as a collector.

At first, my target areas were Chongqing and the southwestern regions, particularly the south of Sichuan and Yunnan, where jadeite was first discovered. Later on, I started to look for old jadeite in antique stores across the nation and also through other collectors. After 2010, I could hardly find satisfying old jadeite in the domestic market, so I visited antique dealers and collectors in Japan, USA and Europe to purchase jade. In addition, I also placed bids for old jadeite in various auction companies such as Sotheby's and Christie's. Over the past 20 years, my jadeite collection has increased remarkably, which consists of more than 10,000 items. These antique jadeite artifacts basically encompass all types of jade wares, which date back to the early Ming Dynasty, the Republic Era, and all the way to the early 1950s and 1960s.

As my collection expanded, I suddenly had a strong desire to thoroughly investigate the place of origin, history and import routes of old jadeite. These years, I explored Myanmar where a lot of jadeite is produced, paid several visits to Tengchong, Baoshan, Dali, Zhaotong in Yunnan and Yibin and Jiangjin in Sichuan, called on local experts, collectors, jade artists and professional associations, collected related written materials, treaded on the paths through which jadeite was imported, and finally gained a general understanding of the origin and history of jadeite.

According to written documentation, jadeite was discovered as early as the Yuan Dynasty. By the Ming Dynasty, a substantial amount of jadeite had been made into goods and wares, primarily accessories for civilians. Most jade wares were circulated across the southwestern regions including Yunnan, Guizhou and Sichuan. In the Qing Dynasty, jadeite was introduced to the royals, and a variety of jade wares were produced. Its processing techniques also largely improved. Like a phoenix reborn from ashes, jadeite finally elevated itself from accessories for civilian use to "imperial jade".

Without a doubt, jadeite wares created a brand new page in the Chinese jade history in modern China. It injected new blood into the development of Chinese jade culture.

Jade is defined as "pretty stone" in "Shuowen Jiezi". For a very long time, Chinese people did not specifically distinguish jade from stone. Over the past 8,000 years of Chinese jade history, ancient Chinese used multiple types of jade, including nephrite like Kunlun Jade, Dushan Jade, Lantian Jade and Xiuyan Jade, as well as agate, crystal, turquoise and quartz.

The great scholar in modern China Zhang Hongzhao said in his book "Shi Ya": when ancient people selected stones, they first looked at "de" and then "fu". "De" means the quality of a stone and "fu" color. Although ancient people used a great variety of jade, they paid no special attention to jade quality, and it is fairly difficult to find jade with great color, gleam and quality at the same time. For jadeite, northerners tend to prefer color over quality. However, in the southwestern regions, especially in Yunnan, some people favor "quality" over "color". The clarity of jade as well as the richness of the color are also two important factors to distinguish superior jade from inferior. The Erhai Lake area in Dali is commonly known as a "kingdom of iridescent jade", where the tradition of wearing jadeite can be dated back to the Qing Dynasty. Civilians all wear Piaohua Jade bracelets and bright green Qiluo Jade earrings for marriage. As such, there are a large number of Piaohua Jade bracelets of high quality in this region. The most famous semi-transparent Piaohua jade bracelet is Duanjia Jade. Northerners and southerners have reached a mutual understanding that the best jade is the kind with both great "colors" and "qualities", such as the well-known Wangjia Jade (imperial jade), which is as precious as diamond. Jade appraisers normally regard this type of jade in a blended color of water and sky. Due to limited transportation, it is a grand and arduous undertaking to climb over Bonan Mountain and cross Jihong Bridge to search for good jade.

The improvement in raw materials presents how the Chinese jade culture has developed and progressed over time. When we reflect upon the Chinese jade ware history, we would find that from the late Neolithic to the Spring and Autumn and the Warring States periods, the majority of jade was produced locally, and Hetian Jade was fairly rare. From the Han Dynasty, as a result of the opening of the trade routes to the Western Regions, an exceeding amount of Hetian Jade was imported to the Central Plains, becoming the main material for Chinese jade wares. In the Ming and Qing Dynasties, jadeite rose to fame and elevated itself from the masses to the royal court.

Historically speaking, jadeite did not receive much attention until at a very late age. As a relatively new type of jade, it is a gem highly treasured in the Western countries.

Early jadeite was primarily composed of white jade, and white jade with patches of green was the most popular among all. Emperor Qianlong loved non-transparent white jade with patches of bright green the most. The clarity of jade was not an important factor until the ruling of Empress Dowager Cixi.

Emperor Qianlong wrote a poem titled "Jingyu Gaojie Yuan", which reads, "As fresh as bamboo, as green as clear water, the jade is enveloped in agleamy splendor. Nothing is as unique as this jade. It's as noble as a man of honor." Emperor Qianlong loved jadeite. According to a statistical report, among all the poems written by Emperor Qianlong, over 50 were dedicated to jadeite.

Antique jadeite wares have different designs, styles and patterns, processed by various techniques. They not only portray folk cultures but also the old royal glamour. At the same time, old jadeite, together with the jade culture and the jewelry culture, forms an international image of the Chinese jade culture.

Since the start of reform and opening-up, there have been many publications about domestic jade wares. However, there are very few on the research of old jadeite. Mr. Gu Fang,a reputable ancient jade researcher, says that among his publications on ancient Chinese jades, there is none discussing jadeite, which is an important branch of the jade culture. When he learned that my humongous collection of old jadeites practically covers all jadeites of different kinds and qualities since jadeites were first introduced to China, he believed that it constituted great materials for researching into the complete history and development of Chinese jadeite arts. Mr. Gu Fang and people at the Cultural Relics Publishing House encouraged me to write and compile a catalogue book fully presenting old Chinese jadeites based on my collection. After communication on several occasions, the Cultural Relics Publishing House and I finally reached an agreement to publish this book.

Old jadeite occupies a glorious place in the Chinese jade ware history. Our goal and reason for publishing this book Early Modern Jadeite is to carry forward and promote the Chinese jadeite culture, anindispensable branch of the Chinese jade culture, and share our knowledge with jadeite lovers.

近代中国翡翠概论

古 方

所谓老翡翠，即指明代、清代以及民国时期用翡翠原石加工成的制品。相对于二十世纪八十年代以来开采加工的新翡翠而言，老翡翠的概念还包括了一部分二十世纪六十至七十年代创汇期生产的翡翠。本书所收录的就是上述不同时期生产并流传至今的老翡翠。翡翠，也称翡翠玉、翠玉、硬玉、缅甸玉，是中国传统玉石的主要品种之一。它的矿物成份是硅酸铝钠，属辉石类，

图 1｜雾露河

硬度 6.5-7，比重约 3.3。1863 年，法国矿物学家德穆尔（Augustin Alexis Damour）对翡翠制品进行了检测，因其硬度大于以透闪石为主的和田玉，而将这种矿物定名为"硬玉"，英文名称为 jadeite 或 jadeite jade。

世界上出产翡翠的国家有危地马拉、美国、日本、俄罗斯和缅甸。目前我们所见的翡翠 95% 来自于缅甸，也只有缅甸的翡翠才能达到宝石级别，具有很高的工艺和珠宝市场价值。缅甸翡翠矿区主要位于缅甸西北部雾露河（又称乌龙河）上游（图 1），属克钦邦帕敢地区，缅北最著名的翡翠聚散城市是密支那，最有名的厂口是勐拱。原生矿带长约

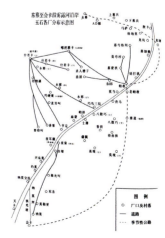

图 2｜东慕至会卡段雾露河沿岸玉石各厂分布示意图（引自张竹邦：《勐拱翡翠经》90 页）

图 3 | 翡翠矿的次生堆积

图 4 | 老厂翡翠原石

1

张竹邦:《翡翠探秘》,云南科技出版社,2005 年。

张竹邦《勐拱翡翠经》,云南科技出版社,2005 年。

2

许慎:《说文解字》卷四上,中华书局,1963 年。"翡,赤羽雀也,出郁林,从羽非声;翠,青羽雀也,出郁林,从羽卒声。"

3

例如:河南辉县琉璃阁战国墓地 M60 出土一对月牙形玉璜,据报道其质料为"澄绿翠绿的硬玉"。硬玉即是翡翠。(见郭宝钧:《山彪镇与琉璃阁》,61 页,科学出版社,1959 年)后经台湾中央研究院历史语言研究所检测,均为透闪石玉,而非翡翠。(见古方:《辉县琉璃阁墓地出土玉器考察》,《考古》2005 年第 8 期)

4

王丽明:《略谈云南出土翡翠》,《收藏家》2012 年第一期。

250 千米,宽约 15 千米,面积三千多平方千米。在这块地方分布着大大小小成百上千个玉石矿场(图 2),分老厂和新厂。老厂玉又称老山玉、老坑玉、砂矿,为天然翡翠原矿脉经外力作用分裂、撞击、滚动、风化而形成的次生堆积,外表光滑,如同大小不一的鹅卵石(图 3),分布于河流两岸山坡、滩地和河床底部,早期发现的翡翠原石都是在河边及老河床底部捡到的。老厂玉都有一层沙壳(即风化层)包裹着,玉的种、色一般不外露,如著名的老厂口料白岩沙和黄岩沙,切开后才能看到玉质(图 4)。老厂矿有麻蒙、会卡、帕敢、龙塘、南水河、木那、育马登等。新厂又称新山玉、新坑玉,即翡翠的原生矿脉,光绪初年被发现,地处干昔山区,凡属龙塘西北的为新山玉。矿脉在地面下约十四五丈深,夹杂于青石层中,块度较大,棱角分明(图 5)。新厂玉主要是种地新,色份也与老厂口玉有所不同[1]。

翡翠本指南方两种鸟名,以红、绿两种艳丽的羽毛而著称,后来被用来命名这种以红翡绿翠为特征的矿物。翡翠一词最早见于汉代文献[2],但直到宋代,文献中所提到的"翡翠",或指颜色,或指鸟羽制作的装饰品,而非玉石原料。在传世的翡翠制品中,在内地未见明代以前之物。曾有考古报告提及汉代以前的墓葬中出土了"翡翠饰品",但后来经检测并非翡翠质地[3]。在云南地区正式考古发掘出土的翡翠实物均属清代,未见清代以前的翡翠制品[4]。但民间老

图 5 | 翡翠新山玉

翡翠行业对有明代翠玉无太大争议，且在云南有较大存世量。尤其在大理（滇西地区），明晚期的一些首饰类翠玉制品，多见于手镯、戒指、发簪、玉佩等。手镯为素器，少工，讲究线条和流线，有圆条圆口、扁条圆口、半圆条圆口、圆条椭圆形口、半圆条椭圆形口、扁条椭圆形口。扁条外圈面多有凹槽，线条流畅漂亮，朴素典雅。偶见竹节形和双龙戏珠形手镯（图6、7 ）。指环的戒面部分多有凹槽。明代翠玉器型多与同时期金银器的风格、器型和纹饰一致。在腾冲翡翠博物馆有明代出土的翡翠实物和相应的墓志铭。其中手镯为圆条圆口，与清代风格一致，只是有的条杆偏细。

图6｜明代竹节形手镯　　　　　　　　图7｜明代双龙戏珠形手镯

根据一些文献记载，最初翡翠原石的发现源于马帮。十三世纪时，腾冲的马帮到缅甸贩货，回来时为了平衡马背上所驮货物重量，顺手在雾露河边捡了几块石头压重。回到腾冲卸货后，这些石头就被随意抛弃在地上，有的裂为两半（另说为马所踏裂），在断裂的石头里人们意外地发现了"碧光灿烂夺目"的翡翠，从而找到了玉矿。这说明翡翠原料大约是元代时发现的[5]。而制作翡翠器物应是从明代才开始的。

翡翠矿场的开采，从元代至今已有七百多年的历史，但自然条件恶劣，只有在旱季才能开采，开采方法十分简陋。每年霜降，滇西一带的采玉人进入缅北地区，到了玉石矿先选无人挖过较有希望的地方，以小树枝或竹一株插下以为标记，然后用焚祭祈求神灵庇护，早得玉石。祭祀后破土动工，二到五人挖一洞，其洞深浅不一，有

5
徐赞周：《缅甸地理志》，
思明日新书局，1932年。

图8 | 开采翡翠矿　　　　图9、图10 | 拣选翡翠原石

的挖到三四丈，方达石层，石层的厚薄疏密不一样，有的很快就能挖到玉石，有的竟四五个月一无所获。矿洞有的在山坡，有的在河边，还有的在山腰。在河边的需要一边挖一边用竹筒拉水，翡翠开采如同一场赌博。现在开始使用挖掘机进行开采，虽然节省了人力，但开采成本也非常高，尤其是玉石的挑拣环节离不开大量的人工劳动，开采过程极为艰辛（图8、9、10）⁶。明代诗人杨慎（杨升庵）的《宝井篇》对开采玉石的恶劣环境、生活情景有着生动深刻的描述："潞江（雾露河）八湾瘴气多，黄草坝邻猛虎坡。编茅打野甘蔗寨，崩磧浮沙曩转河。说有南牙山更恶，髡头漆齿号蛮莫。光挠戛磴与猛连，哑瘴须臾无解药。……得宝归来似更生，吊影惊魂梦犹怕。"⁷

古代腾冲和勐拱两地共称"腾越"，东汉时属永昌郡；"腾越置官，创于元世"，从元代开始，腾越作为中国领土受元朝廷管辖。清乾隆时期《云南腾越州志》载："前明尽大金江内外，三宣、六慰皆受朝命。而腾越且兼戛鸠、蛮莫、勐拱、勐养而有之。"⁸玉石产

6
张竹邦：《翡翠探秘》，云南科技出版社，2005年。
7
杨慎：《升庵遗集》（卷四），天地出版社，2002年。
8
屠述濂 纂修：《云南腾越州志》（文明元、马勇 点校）卷三，云南出版集团、云南美术出版社，2006年。

图11 | 明代翡翠产地及滇缅地区图（来源：《中国历史地图集》）

地勐拱"在朱明之世已隶版籍，延至清乾隆百年后"，仍属"滇省藩篱"的土司辖地，由腾越州管辖，故有"玉出云南"之说（图11）。明正统之后的一百多年间，缅甸翡翠开采是由当地土司阶层统治管理，经营玉器厂，大批华侨进入勐拱地区开采挖掘，使腾越边区玉石业繁荣起来[9]。1885年，英国侵占缅甸之后，勐拱划入缅甸殖民地，因为玉石矿山地域宽阔，难于管理，偷税漏税较多，英国殖民者又不便自己开采，就采用包税的办法，将玉矿的税收招商投标（即"岗税"），招商中标的基本是华人。矿山开采和"岗税"长期由华人来管理。缅甸独立后，相当长的一段时间内延续英国人的办法，玉石的开采与贸易依然由华人控制。毛应德是腾冲华侨向缅政府承包玉石厂"岗税"第一人。张宝廷、寸如东、李寿郁、黄桢庭等都曾以巨额资本承包"岗税"，所有进入市场和工厂的翡翠原石都要"过岗"。开采玉石在当时基本上被腾商承包，故有"上缅甸是云南人的势力"之说。最为知名的翡翠大王张宝廷，在清宣统时期承包经营玉石厂，甚至无偿出资帮助当地土司从英商手中赎回玉石厂厂权，并以雄厚资金向英国政府承包"岗税"[10]。直到1966年，缅甸政府不准私人开矿，将所有的矿产资源收为国有，一切想要开采的场口都要向缅甸政府购买开采权，翡翠原料禁止私下交易，只有经过公盘交易（即"赌石"）才能进行加工、运输和在国内外销售，也就是说，除了翡翠公盘之外出境的的所有卖翡翠原料的行为都被视为走私，也让赌石交易更为官方化。其实，赌石历史非常悠久，明末清初，"穷走夷方急走场"成了腾冲人发家致富的生活方式，他们出走缅甸，带回来一块块翡翠原石论质出售，这就是最初的赌石。有历史记载的则是清代乾隆年间檀萃的《滇海虞衡志》："玉自南金沙江来，江昔为腾越所属，距州二千余里，中多玉，夷人采之，搬出江岸，各成堆，粗矿外护，大小如鹅卵石状，不知其中有玉，并玉之美恶与否。估客随意贸之，运之大理及滇省，皆有玉坊，解之见翡翠，平地暴富矣。其次利虽差而亦赢。最下，则中外尽石本折矣。"[11]这说的就是赌石性质的贸易，也是赌石的起源。"一刀穷，一刀富，一刀开当铺，一刀披麻布"就是对赌石形象的描述。

毫无疑问，最早去缅甸开采、经营翡翠的就是地理位置最有优势的腾冲人。腾冲是距离翡翠开采地最近的地方。明代永乐元年九月（1403年），置腾守御千户所。明正统十年（1445年）设腾冲军民指挥使司，在地理上腾冲已成为控制中缅交通的要冲。古代的"南方丝绸之路"和著名的史迪威公路就经过腾冲直接贯通缅北进入东南亚、南亚抵达印度（图12）。腾冲凭借先天的地理、交通和政治优势，很长一段时间，几乎是缅甸翡翠和其他物品进入中国的唯一通道。明景泰元年（1450年），兵部侍

9
夏光南：《中印缅交通史》，中华书局，1948年。
10
转引自张竹邦《翡翠探秘》。
11
檀萃：《滇海虞衡志》，丛书集成初编，商务印书馆，1936年。

图 12 | 史迪威公路路碑　　　　　　　图 13 | 腾冲城南门内大街（1902 年 G.E.Morrison 拍摄）

12
徐霞客：《徐霞客游记》卷九上，上海古籍出版社，2015 年。"先一石白多而间有翠点，而翠色鲜艳，逾于常石。人皆以翠少弃之，间用掊抵上司取索，皆不用之。余反喜其翠以白质而显，故取之。潘谓此石无用，又取一纯翠者送余，以为妙品，余反见其黯然无光也。今命工以白质者为二池，以纯翠者为杯子。"

13
屠述濂 纂修：《云南腾越州志》（文明元、马勇 点校）卷三，云南出版集团、云南美术出版社，2006 年。

14
寸开泰：《腾越乡土志》，中国文联出版社，2005 年。

郎侯琏筑腾冲石城，来自全国各个省份的南征将士大都落籍腾冲，日后又大规模移民屯田。明末永历帝奔缅，从者数十万，从勐拱运进的玉石到腾冲使这些能工巧匠有了用武之地。明晚期《徐霞客游记》中记载了当时在云南腾冲翡翠流行的盛况，徐霞客还记录了潘一桂送给他两块翡翠玉石的情景，反映了当时已有对翡翠质量的评判标准[12]。清乾隆时，腾冲成为翡翠毛料集散地及加工中心。《云南腾越州志》载："盖大金江内外，万宝鳞萃……皆从腾越进，故州城八宝街，旧讹为百宝街。""今商客之贾于腾越者，上则珠宝，次则棉花。宝以璞来，棉以包载，骡驮马运，充路塞道。今省会解玉坊甚多，磨沙之声，昼夜不歇，皆自腾越至者。"[13]清晚期英国占领缅甸后，腾冲翡翠加工业仍然比较兴旺，成书于光绪三十一年（1905 年）的《腾越乡土志》对其规模有着详细记载："玉工，制朝珠、手镯、簪珥、各玩器，琢磨之声达昼夜、彻通衢。局肆成事者数百人，散处村落者数千家。"翡翠原料从缅甸源源不断进入腾冲，"腾越商人向以走缅甸为多，岁去数百人，有设立号房于新街、瓦城、漾贡者，亦有不设号房年走一次者。""翡翠，非经腾过无由入内，所以腾为翠薮，玉工满千，制为器皿，发售滇垣各行省。上品良玉，多发往粤东、上海、闽、浙、京都。"[14]乾隆、嘉庆年间，腾冲玉石商、玉石工匠组成了"宝货行"行业公会，逐渐在南城八宝街形成经营翡翠成品的店肆（图 13）。1902 年，清政府在腾冲设立腾越海关，进出口贸易开始发展，玉石进口量从1902年的271担，增加到1911年的828担。从八莫到腾冲的道上，经常有七、八千至一万头的马帮运输物资，腾冲海关验货厅每天摆满了大量货驮。更为反映当时翡翠业兴盛的是，货物还在途中，有些玉石商已经将货款转到腾冲，正是"昔日繁华百宝街，雄商大贾挟资来"的写照。腾冲城郊的绮罗、玉璧、大董等地都是重要的翡翠加工地。二十世纪三十年代外国旅行家在腾冲旅行时见到"一个非常大的切割中心云南的腾越，在腾越许多街都有玉石商店和玉石加工的车床。""某长街为玉器行所集，玉工昼夜琢研不辍，余等深夜过之，犹闻蹈轮转床，声声达于百叶窗叶，颇多女工。"[15] 由此可见当时民间翡翠业的繁荣。民国时期，华侨大规模地经营玉石厂，涌现出了毛应德、寸尊福、张宝廷等多位"翡翠大王"（图14），也出现了绮罗玉、段家玉、正坤玉、王家玉、寸家玉和官四玉

图 14 | 寸氏宗祠

等著名商号和上等翡翠代名词。清朝中期至民国初年，从事玉雕作坊的有一百多家，工匠达三千多人。玉石作坊又分解玉行、细花玉匠、玉拱眼、玉光户、大货玉匠、小货玉匠等，翡翠加工已经细化，腾冲成为历史上曾经辉煌一时的"翡翠城"[16]。抗战时期，腾冲沦陷，翡翠产业一度停滞不前。直到二十世纪六十年代末，腾冲以街道为单位的翡翠加工模式开始形成，并集中了一批老艺人，同时组织人员去中原学习玉雕工艺，吸引了广州、北京、上海等地进出口外贸公司或工艺美术厂等来购买毛料或成品。这时期腾冲、上海、北京、广州以及河南等地制作出大量的翡翠精品，大部分都出售给外贸部门或者外商，给国家换来了大量的外汇，促进了当时的国家建设。

腾冲虽为重要的翡翠加工集散地，但是一直以来精加工作坊非常少，当时腾冲主要是制作耳饰、头饰、手镯、挂饰等一些简单的生活用品，工艺较为粗糙（图15、16）。乾隆晚期，源源不断的翡翠经水路进入内地，大量的翡翠毛料和成品源源不断运往北京、扬州、苏州和广东内地，作为翡翠出产地源头的云南工因产品单一、做工粗犷被以宫廷细工为代表的统治阶层所摒弃。而翡翠原料经过清宫造办处玉作、扬州、苏州等地加工，制作成精致的首饰、器皿，受到清统治阶层和民间的推崇，

15
转引自张竹邦《翡翠探秘》一书中，外国旅行家乞伯、美特福的记载。

16
腾冲市文化志编纂委员会、腾冲市文化广播电视体育局编：《腾冲市文化志》，云南出版集团、云南科技出版社，2019年。

张竹邦：《翡翠探秘》，云南科技出版社，2005年。

图 15 | 云南戴翡翠饰品的妇女

图 16 | 云南戴翡翠饰品的儿童

图 17 | 腾冲余料市场

图 18 | 带有切割痕迹的余料

因此越来越多的翡翠原料进入中原。腾冲的翡翠加工工艺仅为西南地区认同，只在云、贵、川等地盛行。到二十世纪四十年代，腾冲翡翠加工业受到战火的波及而衰落，战后重建时，城内外的弹坑是最好的玉石碎料倾倒处，许多价值不菲的边角料被随意埋到了地下，这些边角料里，有很多都是价值连城的翡翠原石。二十世纪五十年代以来，在腾冲大街小巷，凡施工动土都会挖出历史时期大小的翡翠原石及废弃的边角料，真可谓"挖地一尺必得玉"，这从另一方面证实了腾冲从明清至民国是中国西南地区翡翠原料和成品加工、交易的中心，如今翡翠加工遗弃的废料随处可见，形成了今天我们所见到的规模庞大的余料交易市场（图17、18）。

图 19 ｜ 翡翠之路之博南古道　　　　　　　　图 20 ｜ 翡翠之路之马帮

　　翡翠在明末清初已受到官方关注，并进而参与开采和运输。对于翡翠如何进入中原众说纷纭，经过实地考察，最清晰、最便捷的翡翠之路应是翡翠原石经密支那运抵腾冲（旧称"宝井路"），加工成器后，由马帮运输沿着"博南古道"翻越高黎贡山，跨过怒江、澜沧江，过博南山抵达大理（图 19、20）。博南古道也称永昌道，即马帮之道，也是"南方丝绸之路"的重要组成部分，这条马帮之道沿途设置了不少驿站以供来往过客食宿。到大理后，驻云南驿，一条道向北经姚安府过大凉山，再经汉源清溪关入成都；另一条道再向东北过碧鸡关，经昭通"秦五尺道石门关"入川至宜宾，在宜宾这个重要交通枢纽分散至西南地区（图 21、22、23）。翡翠之路蜿蜒穿梭于

图 21、22、23 ｜ 云南盐津"秦五尺道"及"石门关"

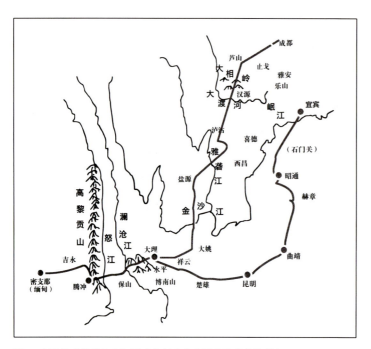

图 24 ｜清代"翡翠之路"图（依据宜宾市博物馆资料绘制）

图 25 ｜清代"东王仙籍图"翡翠插屏
（北京颐和园藏）

崇山峻岭、涧溪河湖之间，长达万里之遥（图 24）。清乾隆后，翡翠在中原逐渐普及，翡翠毛料及成品亦通过宜宾这个翡翠集散地，走长江水路贩运至中原内地和江南。老翠玩家及商人所收的老翡翠大量散布在巴蜀地区，尤其以宜宾及周边为多。这说明当时宜宾是翡翠进入中原的重要集散地和中转站。

翡翠加工虽在云南已有悠久的历史，但也仅限云南境内，尤其是在以腾冲为中心的翡翠之路沿线所在地。从现存的老翡翠收藏中，我们发现最早的翡翠成品多在明晚期。而翡翠制品盛行则是在清代，几乎为朝廷和民间所普及，今天我们所能看到的老翡翠，多为清代产物。这是因为翡翠一开始向内地传播时是走上层路线，明朝时期西南地区的翠玉宝石多作为贡品呈献给朝廷，明中叶高级太监驻守保山腾冲专门采购珠宝。清朝是中国历史上大规模利用翡翠资源的时代，清宫文献中最早记载翡翠的年代是雍正五年（1727 年），为当时云南总督进贡的"翡翠石数珠"。到了乾隆时期，云南进贡的翡翠制品逐渐增多，而清宫造办处、广东、天津、江苏等地也开始生产和进贡翡翠，其品种及造型与宫中流行的和田玉制品并无二致。对于翡翠原料的称呼，则有永昌玉、云南玉、云玉、云产石、滇玉、翠玉、绿玉等[17]。高档翡翠的价格也扶摇直上[18]。翡翠以其艳丽丰富的色彩和晶莹剔透的内质深得女性的青睐，清晚期对翡翠最为痴迷的当属慈禧太后，她常常向各海关、织造等部门索取翡翠贡品，还会定期让人维护她的翡翠首饰，即使颠沛逃难，都不忘关照。湖广总督张之洞投其所好，多次向慈禧进献翡翠，慈禧对于这些翡翠不但爱不释手，而且对其质量和雕工有独到的见解[19]。清宫现藏翡翠制品八百多件，绝大部分是晚清之物（图 25）。宫廷盛行翡翠，也促使民间对翡翠极为推崇，甚至超越了和田玉的地位，成为达官贵人手上最常见的

17
徐琳：《翠华玉意两逢迎——清代宫廷中的翡翠》，《紫禁城》2018年第 5 期。

18
纪昀：《阅微草堂笔记》卷一六，上海古籍出版社，1980 年。"云南翡翠玉，当时不以玉视之，……今则以为珍玩，价远出真玉上矣"。

19
德龄：《我和慈禧太后》，译林出版社，2016。

珍玩。这时期的翡翠主要在北京、苏州、扬州等地加工，用料讲究，雕工精致。翡翠的发展经历了由民间到宫廷，再由宫廷引领民间的过程，从乾隆开始发展，到清末至民国时期，老翡翠的制作和使用也达到了巅峰。

老翡翠的数量众多，种类丰富，包括陈设摆件、器皿、佩玩、文房、用具等五大类。笔者仔细观摩了本书所刊布的七百多件老翡翠制品，拟就其材质的种、水、色，以及琢刻工艺、造型纹饰等问题进行初步的探讨。

一、材质：与辨别和田玉材质不同，翡翠是从种、水、色来选择。"种"即料子的细腻和纯净程度，或矿坑的新老，有些翡翠能够看到颗粒结构，而有些看不到，能看到颗粒结构的翡翠，说明料子比较粗，不够细腻，相对来说质量不高。料子的种从细到粗为玻璃种、高冰种、冰种、冰糯种、糯种、豆种。老翡翠有少量玻璃种、高冰种，以糯种、冰糯种、冰种为主，豆种为普品，其量最大。糯种质地较为细腻，冰糯种近乎于糯种和冰种之间，局部底色已为冰种。冰种质地细腻，晶莹通透。而高冰种和玻璃种，质地细腻纯净，结晶颗粒细腻致密。如一对玻璃种飘阳绿浅浮雕乾隆通宝钱形平安扣，具有玻璃光泽，而且和玻璃一样透明，品质非常细，结晶颗粒致密，颜色纯正、明亮、浓郁、均匀，是翡翠中的极品（图26）。"水"指的就是翡翠的水头，即翡翠的通透程度，也就是透明度。水头足、水头长就是透明度好，种水越好的翡翠其透明度越高、结晶越细腻，行内经常有"几分水"的说法来表达种地水头的好坏。"色"指翡翠的颜色。翡翠色彩艳丽而丰富，讲究浓、阳、正、和（匀和）。浓是指饱和度要高；阳是指翠色的亮丽和耀眼程度；正是指颜色正气，不偏不倚；和是指色与种的调和。

图26｜玻璃种飘阳绿翡翠平安扣

图27｜紫罗兰翡翠手镯

图 28 ｜ 无色翡翠蝙蝠

图 29 ｜ 白底青翡翠扳指

图 30 ｜ 正阳绿翡翠耳坠

图 31 ｜ 苹果绿翡翠手镯

翡翠有绿色、紫罗兰（图 27）、无色（图 28）、白底青（图 29）等。绿又分很多种，有正阳绿（图 30）、苹果绿（图 31）、淡绿（图 32）。色份有高低浓淡，行内用几分色来表达。所谓"天水一色"就是指高种翡翠带色，色俏且阳，种色一体谓之和。老翡翠中还有部分红翡、黄翡巧色，色彩对比鲜明，尤其是质地细腻、艳丽明媚的红翡在雕琢中起到画龙点睛的作用（图 33）。当然一块翡翠中有红有绿更好，这就是翡翠，古称"福寿双全"。值得一提的是，老翡翠中有一种近似和田白玉的白色翡翠，其雕件外观极易与和田白玉件混淆（图 34），就连乾隆皇帝也将一件进贡的白色翡翠鱼式盒错认为痕都斯坦玉器，并写了一首《咏痕都斯坦玉鱼》诗刻于器内。[20]

　　二、琢刻工艺：在翡翠玉器界有"远看造型近看玉，拿起细细看刀工"之说，所谓"刀工"就是翡翠的雕刻技法。从古至今，琢玉工艺基本上都遵循着"选料—设计—制作—抛光"这几道工序，而"制作"工序中的雕刻技法，主要可以分为线刻、浮雕、圆雕、镂雕、链雕、俏雕等几大类。此批翡翠雕刻工艺多种多样，运用了浅浮雕、高浮雕、圆雕、镂空雕、俏雕等工艺。线刻的表现手法有两种，一种是将平面上画样的线条刻去，为阴线刻；另一种是相反的方式，刻去线条之外的部份，图案形成凸起的棱线，

20

徐琳：《翠华玉意两逢迎——清代宫廷中的翡翠》，《紫禁城》2018年第 5 期。

称为阳线刻。这种雕刻方式也常运用在表现人物的头发、动物的毛发、植物轮廓和水浪等细节。翡翠佩玩和用具等类经常采用线刻技法，如寿比南山如意锁牌、双蝠捧寿圆扣、长命富贵如意锁牌均为线刻工艺（图35）。浮雕，介于圆雕与平面绘画之间，是在平面上雕刻出凹凸起伏形象的一种雕塑，它形态各异，能立体形态，能平面形态，既能依附载体，也能独立存在，有浅浮雕和高浮雕之分。陈设摆件、器皿、佩玩和用具中常见浮雕工艺，如清代狮钮活环三足炉器身雕琢成高浮雕（图36），而清代饕

图32 ｜ 淡绿翡翠佩

图33 ｜ 红翡子母猴摆件

图34 ｜ 白翠手镯

图35 ｜ 线刻双蝠捧寿纹翡翠圆扣

图 36 | 高浮雕狮钮活环翡翠三足炉

图 37 | 浅浮雕海屋添筹纹翡翠插屏

饕纹翡翠如意和清代红木座海屋添筹翡翠插屏为浅浮雕工艺（图 37）。圆雕又称立体雕，观赏者可以从不同角度看到物体的各个侧面。它要求雕刻者从前、后、左、右、上、中、下全方位进行雕刻。文房和器皿类均为圆雕工艺，如洗、碗之类的器物（图 38）。镂雕是在浮雕的基础上，镂空其背景部分，在雕刻载体上透雕出各种图案、花纹，有的为单面雕，有的为双面雕，如清代双龙锁牌、双狮戏球镂空佩、翡翠仕女等都采用了镂雕工艺（图 39）。 平面镂空则有剪纸艺术效果。俏雕指的就是巧色的利用，把不同部位的颜色都充分运用到艺术创作中，凸显出整体统一的艺术感，相辅相成。如清代镂空麒麟吐玉书带扣、红翡巧色带扣、巧色螭龙诗文烟壶，巧妙的利用黄翡、红翡巧色巧雕而成（图 40）。"俏"其实就是设计师独到的构思以及取义的巧妙，

图 38 | 圆雕翡翠洗

图 39 | 镂雕双狮戏球纹翡翠佩

灵性的构思可以最大程度的体现翡翠的优势,把整个作品提升一个档次。这个过程考验的是对于翡翠原料的拿捏把控,只有充分了解了原料的色、种、水、结构以及大小,才能做出最好的设计,这是雕刻的巧妙之处。

老翡翠的工艺特点有:1.砣碾:砣为古代碾玉用的圆盘形工具,器物上常常会留有砣具碾琢的工艺痕迹。如葫芦形洗中叶片上留有砣碾细阴线痕迹;荷叶形洗的底部纹饰中,全部阴线皆为精湛的砣碾痕迹,线条流畅细腻,口沿的处理上体现了手动工具时代的最高水准(图41)。在蝠形佩中可见阴刻曲线线条的砣痕痕迹;墨床中的纹饰中也可见与明清常见的浅浮雕一致的砣碾线条。斜坡状砣痕又称"一面坡",就是将砣具偏倾角度,利用其侧刃带动潮湿的解玉砂碾制,使得线痕呈现出一面深、一面浅的斜坡状。如赏瓶瓶口处可见与玉器工艺一致的"一面坡"与"双阴挤阳"砣痕(图42)。2.桯钻和管钻:明清玉雕中,有很多镂雕、透雕作品,它们有一定的厚度,常常形成立体的或多层的纹饰,反面也常能看到管钻或桯钻的痕迹。钻在玉雕作品中是不可少的,钻分为实心钻和管钻两类,实心为桯钻,空心为管钻。如葫芦形水洗半成品中可见到桯钻与管钻去料痕迹(图43),另一件葫芦形洗中,在葫芦藤处留有桯钻去料形成的形状及边角。镂雕中经常能见到桯钻痕迹,比如福禄万代佩镂空处可见到桯钻定位角痕(图44)。还可见不同尺寸管钻去料留下的钻痕。3.掏膛:是琢制玉容器内部的去料和琢磨工艺。在炉、瓶、盒、碗、杯、鼻烟壶等玉容器制作中常用

图 40 | 红翡巧色带扣

图 41 | 留有砣碾细阴线痕迹的葫芦形洗

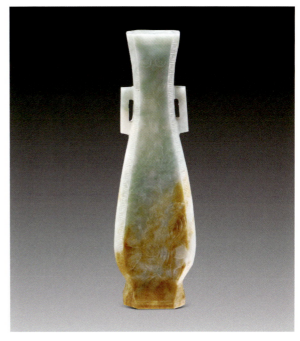

图 42 | 带有斜坡状砣痕的翡翠赏瓶

图 43 | 带有桯钻与管钻去料痕迹的葫芦形水洗

图 44 | 带有桯钻定位角痕的福禄万代纹翡翠佩

图 45 | 磨砂地冰种双龙捧寿纹翡翠锁牌

图 46 | 粗打磨的翡翠方扣

此工艺，使用的掏膛工具有碗砣和钩砣等。4.磨砂：其工艺的特点是具有细小的褶皱，使器表底子更美观，出现在明晚期，如冰种双龙捧寿锁牌体现了当时的磨砂地工艺水准（图45）。5.抛光打磨：指在翡翠作品完成后，用抛光打磨工具配以特殊材料，磨去因制作产生的砣痕，使其表面细腻光滑，是玉雕中很重要的一环，一般分为机抛和手抛。如清代方扣上留有早期粗率打磨的痕迹（图46），而葫芦形洗代表了清代常见的翡翠抛光效果。

图 47 | 烤红翡手镯

三、造型纹饰：1.陈设摆件：用于室内摆设的大小不同的翡翠艺术品。老翡翠摆件的造型多样，有人物、如意、仙子、花插、挂屏、瑞兽等，纹饰题材丰富，多为吉祥题材，如童子、宝莲穿鸭、刘海戏金蟾、海屋添筹、太师少师、辈辈封侯，福禄寿、鸿运当头等。2.器皿：即翡翠容器，并附有圆雕、浮雕、镂空雕等多种纹饰。器型有炉、瓶、壶、觚、碗、杯、盒等。纹饰有龙纹、花鸟纹、福寿三多纹、鼓钉纹、花卉纹。碗和杯基本是素面无纹。3.佩玩：即用玉佩带和手把玩的翡翠雕件，数量最多，有组佩、镯子、耳坠、带钩、扳指、平安扣、花片等等。题材主要有福寿双全、福在眼前、年年有余、苍龙教子、童子拜寿等。纹饰有牡丹花卉纹、鱼龙纹。器型多为方形、圆形或随形而雕。4.文房：明清时期各种文房用品都颇受文人喜爱和关注，如水洗、水盂、印章、印泥盒、笔架、墨床、镇纸等。水洗造型多样，多数为花卉形，有荷叶形、海棠形、蝶耳活环形、葫芦形、桃形洗、随形洗等，少数为圆形、方形。纹饰为荷叶纹、桃纹、螭纹、卷云纹、鱼莲纹、花草纹、瓜果纹、鸟纹、鸭蟹纹、松鹤鹿纹等等。5.用具：多为日常生活用品，如带扣、钮扣、帽正、帽花、簪子、朝珠、提携、瓦子、烟具（烟壶、烟嘴、烟灰碟）、西洋餐具。带扣造型别致多样，有圆扣、方扣、蝠形扣、牡丹花形扣、双环扣、双胜扣、苍龙教子带扣等。扣上多有吉祥纹饰，如竹节纹、如意纹、花纹、螭纹、松鹿纹、并蒂莲纹、寿字纹、喜字纹、寿桃蝴蝶纹、摩羯纹。题材也是丰富多彩，如麒麟吐玉书、福寿双全、海屋添筹、双龙捧寿等。

图 48 涂绿色翡翠扳指

图 49 仿翡翠玻璃带钩

　　老翡翠中还流行烤色和仿翡翠的做假方法。天然的红色翡翠很少，一些红翡作品为人工烤色，在一些褐红色、棕色或褐黄色等翡翠上加矿物颜料，经高温烧烤变成红色，以营造成红翡、黄翡的效果（图47）。翡翠中的绿色一般很难做烤色，但是绿色照样可以做假，如翡翠嵌银套扳指，在扳指内孔壁上先掏出凹槽，然后再凹槽里涂绿色染料，从外表看很像飘绿的翡翠。扳指里面套入的银套的目的就是为了掩盖这种涂色做假方式（图48）。在老翡翠的市场上还会出现仿翡翠，一般是用玻璃制品和近似翡翠的天然石料代替，如这件带钩就是玻璃的，为玻璃调色烧制而成（图49）。

A General Study of Jadeites in Modern China.

Gu Fang

In Chinese, the term "old jadeite objects" refers to objects made of processed jadeites in the Ming Dynasty, the Qing Dynasty and the Republican era. The "old jadeite objects" may also refer to some jadeite objects processed in the 1960s and 1970s for export to make foreign currency, in opposition to those processed from the 1980s on. Old jadeite objects covered in this book were produced in the above mentioned periods and have survived to this day. The jadeite, also known as the "green jade," the "hard jade," and the "Burmese jade," is one of the major types of traditional Chinese gemstone jade. It is a pyroxene mineral mainly consisting of sodium aluminum silicate, with a hardness of 6.5-7 and a specific gravity of about 3.3. In 1863, French mineralogist Augustin Damour examined some jadeite products and found out that the jadeite has a hardness greater than that of nephrite jade, the key component of which is tremolite. He thus named the mineral "hard jade."

Jadeite deposits are mainly found in countries such as Guatemala, the United States, Japan, Russia and Myanmar. Now 95% of the jadeites we see are from Myanmar, and only those from Myanmar have the quality and value of gemstones that meet the standards of the industry and the market. The major jadeite mining area in Myanmar is located in the upper reaches of the Uyu Ricwe (Fig. 1) in Hpakant of the Kachin State. In north Myanmar, Myitkyina is the most famous collection and distribution center, and Mogaung is the most famous source of jadeite. The alluvial region is 250 kilometers long and 15 kilometers wide, covering an area of 3000 square kilometers. Hundreds of jadeite mines (Fig. 2) are built on the primary and secondary deposits in this region. Jadeites that were transported from the primary deposits by external forces, settled again after splits, clashes, and erosion to form the secondary deposits. Jadeites from the secondary deposits have a smooth surface and look like pebbles of different sizes (Fig. 3). They can be found on the slopes or beaches on both sides of the river, or on the river floor. Early discoveries of raw jadeites were all made on the riverside or on the river floor. Jadeites from the secondary deposits are covered with a sandy shell, which is actually an eroded layer. The type and quality of the jadeites cannot be directly seen. For example, the quality of the well-known raw jadeite rocks "white sandstones" and "yellow sandstones" is not revealed before they are cut open (Fig. 4). Secondary deposit mines include Mamon, Hwehka, Hpakant, Nanshuihe, Lone Ton, Manna, Yumadeng, and so on. The primary deposits were discovered in the early years of Emperor Guangxu's reign in the mountainous regions of Kachin. All the mines northwest of Lone Ton are primary deposit mines. The mineral veins are about around 150 meters under the ground, among the layers of limestone. The jadeite rocks are in large pieces and have uneven surfaces (Fig. 5). The jadeites from the secondary deposits are discovered at a later time and the quality is also different from that of those from the primary deposits (Note 1).

In Chinese word for "jadeite" consists of two parts, *fei* and cui, which respectively refer to birds with glorious red and green feathers. Later, the terms are used to refer to red and green minerals. The term *feicui* is first seen in a document from the Han Dynasty (Note 2). Yet in documents before the Song Dynasty, the term *feicui* was used to refer to either colors or decorations made of feathers, instead of the jadeite. In China, no jadeite objects produced before the Ming Dynasty have been discovered yet. An archaeological report mentioned that jadeite jewelry was found in a tomb before the Han Dynasty, but later an examination showed that the object does not have the quality of jadeite (Note 3). All jadeites unearthed in Yunnan in serious archaeological studies are from the Qing Dynasty. No jadeite objects before the Qing Dynasty have been discovered yet (Note 4). In the jadeite business, however, people have the consensus that jadeite objects were already being produced in the Ming Dynasty, and that many jadeite objects from the Ming Dynasty have survived in Yunnan, especially in the area of Dali in west Yunnan. Most of the jadeite objects produced in the late Ming Dynasty were jewelry such as bracelets, rings, hairpins, pendants, etc. These bracelets are not exquisitely decorated or carved, but they have delicate lines and curves. The bracelets can be a circular ring of a rounded stripe, a circular ring of a flat stripe, a circular ring of a semi-rounded stripe, an oval ring of a rounded stripe, an oval ring of a semi-rounded stripe, or an oval ring of a flat stripe. The outside surface of the flat stripes is often carved with simple but elegant and smooth lines. Occasionally we can see bamboo-shaped bracelets and dragons-and-pearl bracelets (Figs 6 & 7). Most of the rings have sockets. The jadeite objects of the Ming Dynasty are similar to the gold and silver objects of the same period in the styles, shapes and decorative patterns. The collection of the Tengchong Museum of Jadeite includes some jadeite objects of the Ming Dynasty along with the epitaph of the tomb from which they were excavated. Among these objects, a bracelet that is a circular

1

Zhang Zhubang: *Secrets of Jadeite,* Yunnan Science and Technology Press, 2005. Zhang Zhubang: *A Guide to Jadeite of Mogaung,* Yunnan Science and Technology Press, 2005.

2

Xu Shen: *Shuowen jiezi* ('Explaining Graphs and Analyzing Characters'), Part One of Volume Four, Zhonghua Book Company, 1963. "Fei is a bird with red feathers that lives in the woods. Cui is a bird with red feathers that lives in the woods."

3

For example, a pair of crescent-shaped jade pendants were excavated in the Warring-State Tomb M60 in the Liuli Tower of Huixian County of Henan. The report claims that its material is "green hard jade." Hard jade is a name of jadeite. (See Guo Baojun: *Shanbiao Town and Liuli Tower,* page 61, the Science and Technology Press, 1959). Later the test of Institute of History and Philology of the Academia Sinica in Taiwan showed that the material was tremolite, not jadeite. (See Gu Fang: "A Study of the Jade Objects Excavated in the Tomb of Liuli Tower in Huixian County," *Archaeology* no. 8, 2005).

4

Wang Liming: "A Brief Introduction to Jadeite Excavated in Yunnan," *Collectors,* no. 1, 2012.

ring of a rounded stripe is similar in style to jadeite bracelets of the Qing Dynasty, except that its stripe is thinner.

According to some records, the caravans of Yunnan played an important role in the discovery of raw jadeites. In the 13th Century, a trading caravan of Tengchong brought commodities from Burma. On the way they randomly picked some rocks on the bank of the Uyu River to balance the load on the horsebacks. When they were unloading back in Tengchong, they threw the rocks away carelessly. Some of the rocks cracked open and the jadeite shining with splendid green lustre was thus seen. (In another record, the rocks cracked when horses trod on them). This was how the jadeite mine was discovered. The story shows that raw jadeite was discovered during the Yuan Dynasty (Note 5). The production of jadeite objects did not start until the Ming Dynasty.

The mining of jadeites dates back to the Yuan Dynasty and has a history of over 700 years. Due to the harsh conditions, the mining could only be operated during the dry season. The mining method was very simple. Every year at the time of Frost's Descent, miners from west Yunnan would flock to the mining region in north Burma. First they would find an area that had not been mined and that looked promising. They would mark the place with a tree or bamboo branch. They would then burn incense and pray for gods' blessings and for the luck to find the jadeite soon. After the ceremony, they would start digging. A team of two to five people would work on one crater. It was uncertain how much they had to dig. Sometimes they had to dig over ten meters before reaching the rocks. The depth and density of the rock layer varied. Sometimes people could find jadeites very soon. Sometimes people dug for four or five months without finding anything. Some of the mines were on the slope, some by the river and some halfway up the mountain. Those who mined by the river had to scoop up water with bamboo tubes while digging. Jadeite mining was a gamble. Now people started using excavators for digging, which saved labor, but the cost of mining is still high. The process of screening raw jadeites needs a great deal of human labor. Mining was indeed hard work (Figs 8, 9, 10; Note 6). The poem "The Gemstone Mine" by the Ming poet Yang Shen (whose courtesy name was Sheng'an) is a vivid portrayal of the harsh environment and life of jadeite mining:

The area of the zigzagging Uyu River is haunted by miasma.

The Yellow Grass Dam is close to the dens of fierce tigers.

The Sugarcane Village is nothing but thatched cottages in the wild.

The winding river carries sand and causes landslides.

They say the Nanya Mountain is an even fearful place,

5

Xu Zanzhou: *A Record of Burmese Geography*. Siming Rixin Book Company, 12932.

6

Zhang Zhubang: *Secrets of Jadeite*. Yunnan Science and Technology Press, 2005.

With the barbarians who shave their heads and paint their teeth. All the diseases and evil spirits are ferocious;

If you are dumbed by the miasma, there's no cure…

He who is back from the mine seems to be coming back to life;

His soul is still troubled and he is haunted by nightmares." (Note 7).

In ancient times, the area of Tengchong and Mogaung was known as Tengyue, which was under the administration of the Prefecture of Yongchang in the Eastern Han Dynasty. The governance of local cheiftains was established in Tengchong during the Yuan Dynasty. From then on, Tengyue was under the administration of the court of Yuan as part of China's territory. According to the *Annals of Tengyue of Yunnan* from the time of Emperor Qianlong of the Qing Dynasty, "During the Ming Dynasty, the court administered the local chieftains on both sides of the Dajinjiang River, including the areas of Jiajiu, Manmo, Tengyue, Mogaung and Mengyang." (Note 8). The jadeite-producing area of Mogaung "was already part of the territory during the Ming Dynasty. Over a hundred years after Emperor Qianlong's reign," it was governed by local chieftains under the administration of the Prefecture of Tengyue. This is why people said "jadeite was produced in Yunnan." (Fig. 11). In the over a hundred years from Emperor Zhengtong's reign on, Burmese jadeite mining was administered by the local hereditary aristocrats. The local aristocrats operated jadeite factories. Many Chinese came to the area of Moguang to mine jadeite. The jadeite industry in the border area of Tengchong flourished. (Note 9).

After the British occupation in 1885, Mogaung became part of the British colony of Burma. Considering the difficulty of administering the immense jadeite mining region and preventing tax evasion, the British colonists, who were not willing to operate the mining themselves, outsourced the business and put the tax revenue of jadeite mines to tender. The bids were usually won by Chinese merchants and for a long time the mining and tax-farming were managed by Chinese. For quite a long time after independence, Burma continued to implement this British policy and Chinese merchants continued to control the mining and trading of jadeite. Mao Yingde from Tengchong was the first Chinese who obtained the tax-farming contract from the Burmese government. Zhang Baoting, Cun Rudong, Li Shouyu, and Huang Zhenting also made great investment to undertake tax-farming. All raw jadeites were taxed before they were shipped to factories or to the market. At the time, almost all jadeite mining was contracted to merchants from Tengchong, and it was said that Upper Burma was under the influence of the Yunnanese. The most well-known merchant was Zhang Baoting, who was dubbed the King of Jadeite. During the reign of Emperor Guangxu, Zhang ran a jadeite factory by contract. He

7
Yang Shen: *Posthumous Collection of the Writings of Yang Shen.* Vol. 4. Tiandi Press, 2002.

8
Tu Shulian, ed. *Annals of the Prefecture of Tengyue* in Yunnan (arranged by Wen Mingyuan and Ma Yong). Volume 3. Yunnan Publishing Group and Yunnan Fine Arts Press, 2006.

9
Xia Guangnan: *A History of the Communication between China and Burma.* Zhonghua Book Company, 1948.

paid the money out of his own pocket to redeem the ownership of the factory from the British merchant for the local chieftain. With abundant funds, he undertook the tax-farming contract from the British government. (Note 10).

In 1966, the Burmese government forbade private jadeite mining. All the mining resources became state-owned. All miners had to purchase the right of mining from the government before any operation. Private trade of raw jadeites was forbidden. All raw jadeites must be bought and sold through public trading (known as "gambling for jadeite") before they could be processed, shipped or sold in and outside the country. In other words, selling raw jadeites abroad without public trading was considered smuggling. Gambling for jadeite thus became an official activity. Gambling for jadeite has a long history. The saying "he who is in urgent need of money goes to Burmese mines" shows the way the people of Tengchong tried to make a fortune at the turn of the Ming and Qing Dynasties. Those who went to Burma would bring back raw jadeites, which were sold at different prices according to their quality. This was the earliest gambling for jadeite. A historical record of gambling for jadeite is found in *Dianhai yuheng zhi* (*A Record of the Local Administration of Yunnan*) by Tan Cui, who lived in the time of Emperor Qianlong of the Qing Dynasty: "Jadeite is mined in the southern reaches of the Jinsha River. The river, once under the administration of Tengyue, is over a thousand kilometers from Tengyue. The river has abundant jadeite. The natives mine the raw jadeites and pile them on the bank. The raw jadeites, which are in the size of pebbles, are covered by a coarse shell. One cannot tell the quality of the jadeite inside or even whether there is jadeite inside at all. Buyers pay what they will and ship what they buy to the jadeite workshops in Dali and Kunming. If good jadeite is found in the rock when it is cut open, the buyer becomes rich. If jadeite of a poor quality is found, the buyer makes a moderate profit, too. The worst thing that can happen is to find nothing but rock inside. In that case, the buyer loses money in the deal." (Note 11). What we see here is the nature as well as origin of gambling for jadeite. A vivid portray of the gambling is seen in this saying: "Some remain poor after cutting the rock but some become rich; some open a pawn shop after cutting the rock, but some lose all their clothes."

There is no doubt that the location of Tengchong was a great advantage for local merchants in jadeite mining and trading. Tengchong is the nearest town to the jadeite mines. In the ninth moon of the first year of Emperor Yongle's reign in the Ming Dynasty (1403), the Thousand-household Fort of Tengchong was established. In the tenth year of the reign of Emperor Zhengtong of the Ming Dynasty (1445), the Commission of Military and Civil Affairs was established in Tengchong. Tengchong became an important spot that controlled the

10
Quoted in Zhang Zhubang: *Secrets of Jadeite.*
11
Tan Cui: *A Record of the Local Administration of Yunnan. Collected Series Part One.* The Commercial Press, 1936

transportation between China and Burma. Both the Southern Silk Road of the ancient times and the famous Stilwell Road pass Tengchong to get to north Burma before they make their way to Southeast Asia and South Asia and reach India (Fig. 12). With its advantages in geography, transportation and politics, for a long time Tengchong was the only way for Burmese jadeites and other commodity to enter China. In the first year of the reign of Emperor Jingtai of the Ming Dynasty (1450), Vice Minister of War Hou Jin built the Stone Fortress of Tengchong. In this expedition to the south, most of the soldiers who came from different provinces of the country settled down in Tengchong. Later the court migrated a great number of farmers here to cultivate the land. At the end of the Ming Dynasty, Emperor Yongli escaped to Burma with tens of thousands of followers including many craftsmen. The jadeites shipped from Mogaung provided chances for these craftsmen to show their skills. *The Travels of Xu Xiake* of the late Ming Dynasty has a record of the popularity of jadeite in Tengchong of Yunnan at the time. Xu Xiake also narrated how Pan Yigui gave him two pieces of jadeite. The story shows that a standard for judging the quality of jadeite was already established at the time. (Note 12).

During Emperor Qianlong's reign in the Qing Dynasty, Tengchong became the center for gathering, distributing and processing raw jadeite. According to the record in the *Annals of the Prefecture of Tengyue in Yunnan,* "tens of thousands of gemstones were gathered from both sides of the Dajinjiang River… All of them were imported through Tengchong. This is why the Street of Eight Treasures in the city became known as the Street of Hundreds of Treasures." "Now merchants trade all kinds of commodities from gemstones to cotton in Tengchong. The roads were packed with mules and horses carrying large pieces of raw jadeite and packs of cotton. Now there are many jadeite workshops in the provincial capital. The sound of grinding is heard day and night. All the jadeites processed in the workshops are from Tengchong."(Note 13). The British occupation of Burma in the late Qing Dynasty did not interrupt the prosperity of the jadeite processing industry of Tengchong. *Tengyue xiangtu zhi (A Record of the Customs in Tengyue),* a book completed in the thirty-first year of Emperor Guangxu's reign (1905), has a description of the scale of production: "In the jadeite workshops, the grinding sound of producing strings of court beads, bracelets, hairpins, ear rings, and all kinds of objects of amusement went on day and night and could be heard all over the city. Hundreds of people dealt with the business in the city and thousands of households dealt with the business in different villages." Raw jadeites kept flowing into Tengchong from Burma. "Most merchants of Tengyue had their businesses in Burma. Hundreds of them travelled to Burma each year. Some of them set up stations in Xinjie, Wacheng and Yanggong. Some of them had no fixed stations,

12

Xu Xiake: *Travels of Xu Xiake,* Part one, Volume Nine. Shanghai Classics Publishing House, 2015. "A kind of stones are white with bright green speckles, different from ordinary stones. This kind of stones are unwanted because there isn't much green color in them. Sometimes people use them to cope with superiors who extort gifts. Pan said the stone was of no value, and gave me another one that was purely green, which greatly impressed me. In comparison, I can see how the white ones are plain and charmless. Now I had the white stone made into two ink stones and the green one made into a cup."

but travelled once every year." "All jadeites were imported through Tengchong and thus jadeites converged in Tengchong. Over a thousand craftsmen here produced the jadeites into different objects to be sold in Yunnan and other provinces. The jadeites of the best quality are often sold to east Guangdong, Shanghai, Fujian, Zhejiang and Beijing." (Note 14). During the reign of Emperors Qianlong and Jiaqing, the jadeite dealers and craftsmen organized a guild of the gemstone industry. Shops that dealt with jadeite products were built one after another in the Street of Eight Treasures in the southern part of the city. (Fig. 13).

In 1902, the Qing government established the Tengyue Customs in Tengchong. Import and export trade was rapidly developed. The import of jadeites increased from 271 loads in 1902 to 828 loads in 1911. On the road between Bhamo and Tengchong, caravans transported goods with seven to ten thousand horses. Every day, the examination room of the Tengchong Customs was filled with piles of commodities. Some jadeite merchants transferred the payment to Tengchong when the commodities were still on the way. This phenomenon reflects the prosperity of the jadeite industry at the time, which is caught by the verses "In those prosperous days of the Street of Hundreds of Treasures, rich merchants flooded here with full pockets." Qiluo, Yubi and Dadong in the outskirts of Tengchong were also important towns of jadeite processing. In the 1930s, a foreign traveler witnessed the "huge center of jadeite cutting in Tengyue of Yunnan. Jadeite shops and jadeite processing lathes can be found on many streets in Tengyue." "A long street is lined up with jadeite processing workshops. The craftsmen work day and night. When I pass the workshops deep in the night, I can still hear the sound of grinding wheels and lathes from behind the blinds of the window. Many of the workers are women." (Note 15). The description shows the prosperity of the private jadeite industry of the time. During the Republican era, Chinese merchants operated factories that processed jadeite on a large scale. The time saw many jadeite tycoons, such as Mao Yingde, Cun Zunfu, Zhang Baoting, and so on (Fig. 14), as well as famous firms such as Qiluoyu, Duanjiayu, Zhengkunyu, Wangjiayu, Cunjiayu, Guansiyu, and so on. The names of these firms became the bynames for high-quality jadeite. Between the middle Qing Dynasty and the early Republican era, there were over 100 jadeite carving workshops and over 3,000 craftsmen. The jadeite workshops were divided into cutting workshops, fine carving workshops, drilling workshops, polishing workshops, large product workshops and small product workshops. The processing industry was highly compartmentalized. Tengchong had its glorious days as the "City of Jadeite" in history. (Note 16).

During the War of Resistance, Tengchong was occupied by the Japanese army and for a

13
Tu Shulian, ed. *Annals of the Prefecture of Tengyue* in Yunnan (arranged by Wen Mingyuan and Ma Yong). Volume 3. Yunnan Publishing Group and Yunnan Fine Arts Press, 2006.

14
Cun Kaitai: *A Record of the Customs in Tengyue.* The CFLAC Press, 2005.

15
The record of a foreign traveler, quoted in Zhang Zhubang: *Secrets of Jadeite.*

16
A Record of the Culture in Tengchong City. Ed. The Editing Committee, and the Tengchong Bureau of Culture, Broadcasting, Television and Sports. Yunnan Publishing Group and Yunnan Science and Technology Press, 2019.
Zhang Zhubang: *Secrets of Jadeite.* Yunnan Science and Technology Press, 2005.

time the jadeite industry was at a standstill. In the late 1960s, a street-based mode of jadeite processing was formed in Tengchong. A group of old artisans were gathered here. Workers were organized to study the techniques of jade carving in Central China. Foreign trade companies and factories of crafts from Guangzhou, Beijing, Shanghai, etc. were attracted here to purchase raw jadeite or jadeite products. During this period, a large number of high-quality jadeite products were produced in Tengchong, Shanghai, Beijing, Guangzhou and Henan. Most of these products were sold to departments of foreign trade or to foreign merchants. The sales made a great deal of foreign currency for the state, which fueled the construction of the state at the time.

Although Tengchong had been an important center for gathering, distributing and processing jadeite, it did not have many workshops of high-quality craftsmanship. At the time, products of Tengchong were mainly simple objects of daily use, such as earrings, headdresses, bracelets, pendants, etc. The craftsmanship was plain and simple. In the last years of Emperor Qianlong's reign, a great quantity of raw jadeite and jadeite products were shipped by water to Beijing, Yangzhou, Suzhou and Guangdong. The monotonous and rough jadeite products from Yunnan, the source of raw jadeite, were abandoned by the ruling class, which favored the refined, exquisite products of the court-serving craftsmen. The raw jadeites were processed by the jade workshops of the Imperial Office of Manufacture of the Qing Dynasty, as well as the workshops in places such as Yangzhou and Suzhou, and were made into exquisite jewelry and objects, which were adored by both the ruling class and the commoners. Thus, an increasing amount of raw jadeite was shipped into the central plains. The jadeite craftsmanship of Tengchong was only appreciated in southeast China, and the products were only sold in places such as Yunnan, Guizhou and Sichuan.

In the 1940s, the jadeite industry in Tengchong declined because of the war. In the post-war years, the shell craters were the ideal sites for dumping jadeite remnants. Many valuable jadeite remnants, including some raw jadeites of great value, were carelessly buried. From the 1950s on, jadeite remnants and raw jadeites were often unearthed in the construction sites all over the city of Tengchong. As the saying goes, "Dig a foot, and you will find jade." This phenomenon is the evidence that Tengchong had been the processing and trading center of raw jadeite and jadeite products in southwest China in the Ming Dynasty, the Qing Dynasty and the Republican era. Now the remnants from jadeite processing can be found everywhere and a large market of jadeite remnant trading has been formed (Figs 17 and 18).

Jadeite attracted official attention as early as the turn of the Ming and Qing Dynasties. The government participated in the mining and transportation of the gemstone. Different stories are told about how jadeite was transported to China, but on-the-spot investigations show the most obvious and most convenient jadeite trading route: The raw jadeites were transported via Myitkyina to Tengchong (the road was known in the past as the Baojing Road), where the jadeite was processed. The caravans then shipped the jadeite products along the Ancient Bonan Route, going over the Gaoligong Mountain, crossing the Nujiang River and the Lancang River, and passing the Bonan Mountain, to Dali. (Figs. 19 and 20). The Ancient Bonan Road, also known as the Yongchang Road and the Road of Caravans, is an important part of the Southern Silk Road. Many posts were built along the Road of Caravans to provide travelers with boarding and lodging. When the road reached Dali, the site of Yunnan Post, it was split into two: One going north to Chengdu via the Yaoan Prefecture, the Daliang Mountain, Hanyuan, and Qingxiguan, the other going northwest to Yibin, via Bijiguan, Zhaotong, and the "five-foot-wide road" and Shimenguan built in the Qing Dynasty. The goods were then shipped to different places of southwest China via Yibin, the important hub of communication. The Jadeite Road winding over mountains, through valleys, and across streams and rivers, went for as long as five thousand kilometers. (Fig. 24). From the reign of Emperor Qianlong on, jadeite gradually became popular in China. Raw jadeite and jadeite products were shipped by waterway from Yibin, the jadeite trading center, to the central plains and the middle and lower reaches of the Yangtze River. Collectors and merchants of old jadeite have found a great number of old jadeite objects in Sichuan, and especially in the vicinity of Yibin. This is evidence that Yibin was an important trading center and freight station for the transportation of jadeite to China.

The Jadeite processing industry has a long history in Yunnan, but it was only developed within the province, and especially in the area along the Jadeite Road centering on Tengchong. In present-day old jadeite collection, the earliest jadeite products date back to the late Ming Dynasty. The jadeite products didn't come into fashion until the Qing Dynasty, when jadeite was popular in the court and among the commoners. Most of the old jadeite objects we see today were products from the Qing Dynasty. This is because from the beginning jadeite products were targeted at the upper class. During the Ming Dynasty, jade and gemstones from southwest China were presented to the court as tributes. In the middle of the Ming Dynasty, high-ranked eunuchs were stationed in Baoshan and Tengchong to purchase gemstones. The Qing Dynasty was a time when the resources of jadeite were fully used. The earliest reference to it in the documents of the Qing palace dates back to the fifth year or Emperor Yongzheng's reign (1727), which is a record of the tribute of "several jadeites" paid by the governor of Yunnan.

During the reign of Emperor Qianlong, the number of jadeite products presented to the court by Yunnan increased progressively. The Imperial Office of Manufacture as well as workshops in Guangdong, Tianji, Jiangsu, etc. also started producing jadeite objects for the court. The types and design of these jadeite products were the same as those of the nephrite jade products popular in the palace. Raw jadeite was referred to as Yongchang jade, Yunnan jade, Yun jade, Yunnan-produced jade, Dian jade, *cui* jade and green jade, etc. (Note 17). The price of high-quality jadeite soared.(Note 18).

With gorgeous, rich colors and sparkling, translucent quality, jadeite was loved by women. In the Late Qing Dynasty, Empress Dowager Cixi was well known for her fascination with jadeite. She often asked different departments such as the customs, the imperial office of embroidery, etc., for gifts of jadeite. She assigned servants to take care of her jadeite jewelry, which she never forgot even when she was on the run. Zhang Zhidong, Governor of Hunan and Hubei, knew about her love for the gemstones and often gave her presents of jadeite. The empress dowager loved these presents dearly, and she made some perceptive comments on the quality and art of the jadeite objects. (Note 19). The Qing palace had a collection of over 800 jadeite products, most of which were produced in the late Qing Dynasty (Fig. 25). The popularity of jadeite in the palace led to the love of the gemstone in the whole society. Jadeite became even more popular that nephrite jade, and jadeite objects were often seen in the collection of aristocrats. In this period, jadeite was mainly processed in Beijing, Suzhou and Yangzhou. The products were made of high-quality raw jadeite with exquisite skills and art. The love of Jadeite rose among the commoners and later attracted the interest of the court. Then the fashion in the court boosted the popularity of jadeite in the whole society. From the reign of Emperor Qianlong on, the processing and use of old jadeite continued to develop and reached the pinnacle in the late Qing Dynasty and the Republican era.

A great number of old jadeite objects have survived with a great variety of types, which include five major categories: ornaments, vessels, accessories, items of stationery, and items of daily use. After a close examination of the over 600 old jadeite objects in this book, the author wishes to have a preliminary investigation of the quality, transparency, color of the material, as well as the issues of the carving craftsmanship, the designs, and the decorative patterns.

I. The material. The material of jadeite is assessed in a different way from the assessment of nephrite jade. It is examined in terms of its quality, transparency and color.

The quality of the jadeite refers to the degree of fineness and purity of the material, or whether the materials are from primary or secondary deposits. Some jadeite shows its grain

17

Xu Lin: "Jadeite in the Qing Palace" *The Forbidden City*, no. 5, 2018.

18

Ji Yun: *Notes in the Cottage of Close Observation*, Volume 16, Shanghai Classics Publishing House, 1980. "Jadeite is mined in Yunnan. At the time it was not considered as a jade... Now it is considered a precious gemstone, of a value greater than that of jade."

19

Der Ling: *Two Years in the Forbidden City*, Yilin Press, 2016.

structure and some does not. The jadeite that shows too much of its grain structure is not fine enough, and does not have a high quality. The degrees of the fineness of the material are described with the following terms in order from the highest to the lowest level: the "glassy quality", the "high-rank icy quality," the "icy quality," the "icy-waxy quality," the "waxy quality," and the "coarse quality." Only a few old jadeite objects have the "glassy quality" and the "high-rank icy quality." The "icy," "icy-waxy," and "waxy" jadeite is the most common high-quality jadeite. The coarse jadeite objects are sold in the greatest number and for a moderate price. The waxy jadeite has a relatively fine quality. The icy-waxy jadeite has a fineness between that of waxy and icy jadeite, and is often partly icy. The icy jadeite has a very fine quality, and is clear and translucent. The glassy and high-rank icy jadeite is of great purity, and is fine and close in texture with tiny crystal grains. An example of jadeite of such quality is the pair of glassy-jadeite ring pendants with green speckles in the form of Qianlong coins. The pendants feature glassy luster and transparency, fine texture, and closely structured crystal grains. Their color is pure, bright, rich and even. They are jadeite objects of the highest grade (Fig. 26).

The transparency of jadeite refers to the degree of its clearness. The clearer and more transparent the jadeite is, the finer texture and the higher quality it boasts. In the jadeite business, the grade of jadeite is judged in terms of the "percentage of transparency."

Color is another standard for assessing the grade of jadeite. Jadeite is gorgeously and brightly colored. The color of high-quality jadeite is assessed in terms of its richness, brightness, evenness and harmony (that is, how the color fits the texture of the jadeite). The colors of jadeite can be green, violet (Fig. 27), colorless (Fig. 28), white with green speckles (Fig. 29), etc. The colors of green jadeite can be further divided into bright green (Fig 30), apple green (Fig 31), and light green (Fig. 32). In the jadeite business, the shades of colors are described in terms of the "percentage" of the color. The term "the merged color of water and sky" is used to describe high-quality jadeite with a bright and rich color, and with the color in harmony with the texture. Some old jadeite objects are red or yellow. These colors are bright and vivid. In jadeite carving, the color of red jadeite with a fine quality and a bright luster gives the work a unique artistic charm. The red and green jadeite is even more valuable, and is known as "the blessing of fortune and longevity" in ancient times. It is worth noting that some old jadeite objects are white and are thus easily confused with nephrite jade objects (Fig. 34). Even Emperor Qianlong once mistook a white jadeite fish-shaped box, a gift to the court, for Kestunstein jade. He composed a poem "Ode to the Kestunstein Jade Fish," which was inscribed on the inside of the box. (Note 20).

20
Xu Lin: "Jadeite in the Qing Palace" *The Forbidden City*, no. 5, 2018.

II. The carving craftsmanship. As a saying in the jadeite business goes, when one assesses a jadeite object, "one should examine the form and shape from afar, examine the quality of its material near, and examine the carving craftsmanship closely with the object in hand." The carving craftsmanship refers to the art and technique of jadeite carving. From ancient times to this day, jade processing always includes these procedures: raw material selection, design, production, and polishing. The carving techniques in the procedure of "production" include line carving, relief carving, subtractive carving, modeling, chain carving, "clever carving," etc. This collection of jadeite objects feature a great variety of carving techniques, including low-relief carving, high-relief carving, modeling, subtractive carving, "clever carving," and so on.

The line carving includes two types: Engraved line carving, which is known in Chinese as the *yin* line carving, is to cut lines into the surface. Embossed line carving, which is known in Chinese as the *yang* line carving, is to cut off all the materials except for the intended lines, so that the lines stand out in relief on the surface. The latter is often used to carve people's hair, animals' fur, the shape of plants, waves of water, etc. Line carving is very common in jadeite accessories and items of daily use. The examples of line carving can be seen in the jadeite *ruyi*-shaped plate with line-carved pattern of the Southern Mountain, a symbol of longevity, the jadeite button with line-carved symbols of blessing and longevity, the jadeite *ruyi*-shaped plate with line-carved symbols of longevity, etc. (Fig. 35).

The relief is a form that is situated between modeling and painting, with the carved image standing out on the surface. The relief has various forms. It can be two-dimensional or three-dimensional. It can be part of a work, or stand as an independent work. The relief includes low-relief and high-relief. The carving technique is very common in ornaments, vessels, accessories and items of daily use. The Jadeite tripod censer with a lion-shaped knob and movable rings from the Qing Dynasty (Fig. 36) is an example of high-relief carving. The jadeite ruyi scepter with a carved mythic beast and the jadeite table screen with the relief design of a house in sea waves, both from the Qing Dynasty (Fig. 37) are examples of low-relief carving.

The modeling technique is used to carve round sculptures that can be seen from all sides. The carver needs to work on all sides of the object. Items of stationery and vessels, such as brush washers and bowls (Fig. 38), are carved with the modeling technique.

The subtractive carving is produced on the foundation of the relief, by hollowing out its base to create variousdesigns and patterns. Some works of subtractive carving are one-sided and some are double-sided. For example, the technique of subtractive carving can be seen in the two-dragon lock-shaped plate, the pendant with lions-and-ball pattern in openwork, and the jadeite beauty from the Qing Dynasty (Fig. 39). The subtractive carving on the surface can create the artistic effect of traditional Chinese paper cutting.

"Clever carving" refers to the carving that takes full advantage of the colors of the material in different parts to create a unified artistic effect, with different parts of the work echoing each other. For example, the belt buckle with the hollowed-out pattern of a mythic beast holding a book in mouth, the red jadeite belt buckle, the snuff bottle with carved dragon and poetry from the Qing Dynasty are carved with clever use of the yellow or red colors in the material (Fig. 40). The term "clever" means the clever planning in the design. An ingenious design fully reveals the beauty of jadeite and brings the work to a higher level. This process tests the designer's understanding and control of the raw jadeite. An excellent design is based on a full understanding of the quality, color, transparency, structure and size of the material. This is what's "clever" about the carving.

The old jadeite objects feature marks of the following processing techniques:

1. Use of the stone-roller. The stone roller is a plate-shaped tool used in ancient times to grind jade. Marks of the use of the stone roller can often be seen on jade objects. For example, the fine lines on the leaf of the gourd-shaped brush washer are marks left by the stone roller. The smooth and fine engraved lines in the decoration at the bottom of the lotus-leaf-shaped brush washer are marks of skillful use of the stone roller. The way the mouth of the vessel is ground shows the highest standard in the time of hand-operated tools. (Fig. 41). Curved cut-in lines left by the stone roller can be seen in the bat-shaped pendant. In the decoration on the ink stand, we can also see lines left by the stone roller, which are similar to those often found in the low-relief of the Ming and Qing Dynasties. The slanted marks of the stone roller are known as the "one-sided slopes." These marks, relatively deep at one end and relatively shallow at the other, were made when the stone roller was turned at an angle to grind the object with the damp stone on the side of the roller. For example, the marks of "one-sided slopes" and the marks of an embossed line between two engraved lines can be seen at the mouth of the vase, which are similar to the marks seen on jade objects. (Fig. 42).

2. Use of awl drills and tubular drills. Many works of jade carving in the Ming and Qing Dynasties are made with subtractive carving and fretwork. In these works, three-dimensional or multi-layered decorative patterns are carved on the often thick base. Marks of drilling can often be seen at the back of the works. Drilling is an indispensable technique in jade carving. Two kinds of drills are used in the technique: awl drills and tubular drills. For example, the marks of cutting left by the awl drill and the tubular drill can be seen in the unfinished gourd-shaped

brush washer. (Fig. 43). In another gourd-shaped brush washer, the shapes and edges left by the awl drill can be seen on the vines of the gourd. The marks left by the awl drill are often see in subtractive carvings. For example, the mark of alignment left by the awl drill can be seen in the pendant with auspicious patterns. (Fig. 44). The marks of cutting left by tubular drills of different sizes can also be seen.

3. Hollowing. Hollowing is a grinding technique to cut off the materials from the inside of raw jade, in the production of jade vessels such as incense burners, vases, boxes, bowls, cups, snuff bottles, etc. The tools used include the bow-shaped grind and the hook-shaped grind.

4. Frosting. The feature of this effect is the tiny folds that give the base of the object an artistic look. This technique appeared in the late Ming Dynasty. For example, the pendant with the design of dragons and symbols of longevity shows the high-standard of the frosting technique of the time (Fig. 45)

5. Polishing. When a jadeite product was finished, it would be ground on the polishing tool with special materials to remove the marks of the stone roller and to make the surface fine and smooth. This was an important procedure in jade carving. The objects could be polished by hand or by machine. Marks of rough grinding can be seen on the jadeite buckle from the Qing Dynasty. (Fig. 46). The gourd-shaped brush washer represents the polishing effect that was common in the Qing Dynasty.

III. Decorative patterns. 1. Ornaments: jadeite artworks of different sizes to be exhibited in the room. The old jadeite ornaments come in a great variety of shapes, such as figures, *ruyi* scepters, immortals, flower pads, hanging screens, auspicious animals, etc. The decorative patterns on the ornaments are mostly auspicious motifs, such as children, lotus with ducks, Liu Hai teasing the golden toad, birds bringing chips to the house in sea waves, the elder and younger lions, a young monkey on an old money's back, blessings of fortune, emolument and longevity, great fortune overhead, etc. 2. Vessels. Jadeite vessels are decorated with round carving, relief carving, subtractive carving, etc. The vessels include incense burners, vases, kettles, bowls, cups, boxes, etc. The decorative patterns include dragons, flowers and birds, auspicious patterns, drum nails, flowers, etc. Bowls and cups usually have a plain surface without decoration. 3. Accessories: carved jadeite objects, which people can wear to match their clothing or play in hand. There are a great number of jadeite objects of this type, including pendant sets, bracelets, earrings, belt buckles, thumb rings, good-luck charms, small carved jadeite pieces, etc. The decorations are often motifs such as the blessing of fortune and longevity, blessings before the eyes; abundance every year; the blue dragon teaching his son; children wishing for longevity, etc. The decorative patterns include: peonies, fish and dragons, etc. The shapes of these jadeite objects are often square, circular or oval. Some were carved based on the shapes of the raw materials. 4. Items of stationery. In the Ming and Qing Dynasties, men of letters loved and had interest in all items of stationery, such as brush washer, water basin, seals, seal paste boxes, brush stands, ink stands, paperweights, etc. The brush washers were made in a great variety of shapes; most of them are in the shapes of flowers, lotus leafs, crab-apple flowers, butterflies, rings, gourds, peaches, or abstract irregular shapes. A few of them are circular or square. The decorative patterns include lotus leaf, peach, dragon, cirrus clouds, fish and lotus, flowers and grass, fruit and vegetables, birds, ducks and crabs, pine trees, cranes, deer, etc. 5. Items of daily use, such as belt buckles, buttons, hat decoration, hairpins, court beads, shoehorns, smoking tools (snuff bottles, pipes, ash trays, etc.), European-style tableware, etc. The belt buckles have various and interesting shapes, such as circular buckles, square buckles, bat-shaped buckles, peony-shaped buckles, double-ring buckles, *shuangsheng* buckles, buckles with the "blue dragon teaching his son" pattern. The buckles are decorated with auspicious patterns, such as the bamboo patterns, the ruyi patterns, the flower patterns, the dragon patterns, the pine tree and deer patterns, the paired lotus patterns, the longevity patterns, the happiness patterns, the peach and butterfly patterns, the double-fish patterns, etc. The decorative motifs are varied, including the mythic beast holding a book in mouth, the double blessings of fortune and longevity, birds bringing chips to the house in sea waves, two dragons encircling longevity, etc.

The counterfeiting methods of "baked colors" and jadeite imitation are common in the old jadeite business. Natural red jadeite is very rare. Some red jadeite works are man-made. When maroon brown, or brownish yellow jadeites with added mineral colors are heated in high temperature, they can be turned red. It is difficult to produce the green color in jadeite by the method of "baking," but counterfeits can be made in a different way. For example, the jadeite thumb ring with the inlaid silver inside was made in this way: grooves were carved in the inside of the ring, which were filled with green colors. From the outside, it looks like jadeite with green speckles. The inlaid silver layer was to cover the counterfeiting (Fig. 48.) Imitated jadeite often appears in the market of old jadeite. Usually glass or other natural minerals that resemble jadeite are used in place of jadeite. For example, this belt buckle is made of glass, by coloring and heating. (Fig. 49).

中国老翡翠

十七至二十世纪

中国翡翠艺术

图版

EARLY MODERN CHINESE JADEITE

中国老翡翠 十七至二十世纪中国翡翠艺术·上

陈设摆件

001 清　冰种三色麒麟送子

高 69.3 毫米　宽 67.5 毫米　厚 19.5 毫米

◆ 冰种，晶莹通透，白、绿、黄三色，色彩
丰富。麒麟前腿伸直，后腿作蹬状，双眼圆睁，
全身阴刻鳞甲，脚踏祥云，背上骑一怀抱孩
童的女子，面部柔和。寓意"麒麟送子"。

002 清　冰糯种阳绿乳姑不怠

高 74.7 毫米　宽 41.3 毫米　厚 20.4 毫米

◆ 冰糯种，质地细腻，色泽莹润，飘阳绿。左面为一老者坐在椅凳之上，旁边站一妇女，上衣左襟分开，左乳外露，正喂老者吃奶，妇女右手下方一嗷嗷待哺的孩童。

这件作品表现的是二十四孝中的典故"乳姑不怠"。"乳姑不怠"讲述了唐代崔山南家已是做祖母的媳妇用乳汁孝养已经是曾祖母的婆婆，且不懈怠的孝行故事。

沉静，头梳高髻，身形纤细秀美。身着长裙，裙裾折转飘舞，衣纹刻划流畅自如，背一花篮，花篮外阳绿巧色桃子高过头顶，身旁仙鹿回首凝望。麻姑献寿寓意吉祥长寿之意。

003 清　冰糯种阳绿麻姑献寿

高 134 毫米　宽 49 毫米　厚 23 毫米

◆ 冰糯种，玉质细腻，色泽莹润，带阳绿。麻姑开脸端庄，表情沉静，头梳高髻，身形纤细秀美。身着长裙，裙裾折转飘舞，衣纹刻划流畅自如，背一花篮，花篮外阳绿巧色桃子高过头顶，身旁仙鹿回首凝望。麻姑献寿寓意吉祥长寿之意。

004 清　冰糯种飘绿凤鸟

高 143 毫米　宽 59 毫米　厚 46 毫米

◆ 冰糯种，质地细腻，色泽莹润，飘绿色。圆雕双鸟，雌鸟局部巧色黄翡，站立于山石之上，双目圆睁，身形矫健，羽翼收于腹部两侧，颈部一圈和羽翼刻阴线纹饰，幼鸟憨态可掬，依偎于雌鸟腹部，昂首衔灵芝。

005 清　糯种三色凤鸟

长 175 毫米　高 83 毫米　厚 23 毫米

◆ 糯种，质地细腻，色泽莹润，绿、黄、白三色，色彩丰富。圆雕凤鸟，呈站立状，翅上雕刻扇形羽毛，双翅收于背部两侧。长尾上翘，羽分两缕支于地，利爪前蹬，赋予了力量感。

006 清　冰种帆船摆件

长 95 毫米　高 106 毫米　厚 7.6 毫米

◆ 冰种，质地细腻，色泽莹润，淡绿色。船
以圆雕、透雕技法雕琢而成。船头一男子前
屈右腿，奋力划桨；中间一男子扬帆竖起信
号旗；船尾一女子配合船头男子划桨，桨一
前一后相互呼应；整器人物寥寥几笔刻画，
帆上卷云纹、缆绳上斜棱纹清晰可见，动态
十足。

007 清 糯种阳绿帆船摆件

高 82 毫米　宽 67.5 毫米　厚 8 毫米

❖ 糯种,质地细腻,色泽莹润,飘绿。以镂雕和圆雕工艺雕琢而成。船头两端翘起,船头男子稍前屈右腿,奋力划桨;船尾男子指示方向;人物构图简略,均身着斜襟紧袖短衫,帆上刻宽阴刻线,有一帆风顺之意。

008 清 糯种狮吼观音

高 175 毫米　宽 72 毫米　厚 60.6 毫米

◆ 糯种，色泽莹润，浅绿色。观音面相慈善，神态安详，肌肤丰腴，垂发肩后，衣带飘扬。双手环抱一只娇憨可爱的小狮子。

009 清　冰糯种紫罗兰仕女

高 165 毫米　宽 64 毫米　厚 58 毫米

◆ 冰糯种，质地细腻，色泽莹润，通体紫罗兰色。圆雕一身姿秀美的仕女，云髻高耸，裙裾翩翩，双手前伸，似捧盘状。人物开相精湛，姿态极美。

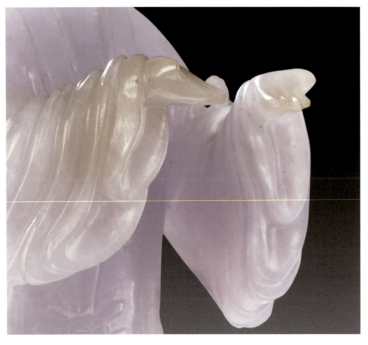

010 清 糯种盆景仕女（一对）

高 215 毫米　宽 112 毫米　厚 34.4 毫米

◆ 糯种，质地细腻，色泽莹润，飘绿。以镂雕和圆雕工艺雕琢出一对仕女与山石、盆景相依相偎、动静结合的曼妙景致，仕女面带微笑，云髻高耸，身着长裙，一手触摸花盆，一手执扇翘兰花指。

仕女脚下和身旁的怪石洞眼相通，巧色阳绿的枝叶更是为其添上一抹亮色，生动传神。

011 清　糯种三色执扇仕女（一对）

左　带座高 200 毫米　宽 102 毫米　厚 37 毫米
右　带座高 210 毫米　宽 80 毫米　厚 40 毫米

◆　糯种，质地细腻，色泽莹润，白、绿、紫三色，色彩丰富。圆雕仕女一对，带鎏金底座。女子云髻高耸，眼眉清秀，长裙衣褶间转折流畅。左边仕女身体右倾，一手自然垂下，一手执扇；右边仕女身体左倾，右手上翘兰花指，左手执扇下垂，两人似在窃窃私语。

012 清　冰糯种飘绿如意观音

高 168 毫米　宽 49.6 毫米　厚 40 毫米

◆ 冰糯种，质地细腻，色泽莹润，飘绿。圆雕观音，发髻高耸，开脸端庄慈祥，腰束贴体罗裙垂落于地，衣带垂于身前，裙摆作飘动状。观音左手执灵芝如意，右手持念珠自然下垂。

013 清　冰种舞剑仕女

高116毫米　宽60毫米　厚24毫米

◆ 冰种，质地细腻，晶莹透亮，淡绿色。雕琢一舞剑仕女，面部清秀坚毅，身着对襟宽袖长袍，衣带飘飘垂到脚边，裙摆作飘动状，双手持剑，作舞剑状，左侧一只凤鸟立于山石之上，回首而望，尾翼下垂。

014 清　糯种紫罗兰净瓶观音

高 195 毫米　宽 63 毫米　厚 36 毫米

◆ 糯种，质地细腻，色泽莹润，通体蓝紫色。观音发髻高耸，发丝
清晰可辨，双目微闭，法相端庄，面部饱满，直鼻丰唇，手持净瓶，
身着广袖长袍，衣褶雕琢层次分明。

015 清　糯种紫罗兰舞姿仕女

高 160 毫米　宽 80 毫米　厚 42 毫米

◆ 糯种，质地细腻，色泽莹润，通体紫罗兰色。立体圆雕一仕女，面容清秀，挺鼻小嘴，云鬟高髻，发丝清晰可见。身姿秀丽，身着广袖长裙，肩披长巾，腰系卡带，裙摆随风卷起。女子款款而立，手执拂尘，衣带飘飘延伸到脚面。

016 清　糯种飘蓝麻姑献寿

高 220 毫米　宽 130 毫米　厚 40 毫米

◆ 糯种，质地细腻，色泽莹润，淡蓝色。圆
雕麻姑开脸端庄，表情恬静，身形纤细秀美，
身着对襟长裙，领口处以阴刻线雕琢纹饰。肩
披长巾，裙裾折转飘舞，麻姑手执如意灵芝，
侧后方仙鹿鹿角高耸，回首凝望。整件器物
雕琢细致入微，工艺极为精湛，为典型的宫
廷器代表作。

017 清　冰糯种阳绿昭君出塞

长 78 毫米　高 83 毫米　厚 22 毫米

◆ 冰糯种，质地细腻，色泽莹润，飘阳绿。在构图上，昭君、胡人和马的布局充分利用了原料特性，人物之间有呼应，昭君骑在马上，鬓发高耸，身披斗篷，着长裙，怀抱琵琶，回首凝望，胯下骏马双目圆睁，头微微昂起，四肢矫健有力，以阴刻线刻画马的鬃毛，尾部下垂侧收，一胡人牵着马缓缓前行。

018 民国　糯种红翡巧色观音立像

高 355 毫米　宽 138 毫米　厚 80 毫米

◆ 糯种，质地细腻，色泽莹润，带红翡。圆雕观音立于莲座之上，法相庄严，身穿裟衣，右手持念珠，自然垂下，左手作与愿印。莲座前后浮雕和阴刻如意纹，镂雕巧色黄翡火焰纹背光，表示佛光普照四方。

019 清　冰种阳绿凤凰盖盒（一对）

长 112 毫米　高 113 毫米　厚 46.3 毫米

◆ 冰种，质地细腻，温润透亮，通体阳绿。凤凰呈站立状，昂首挺胸，弯嘴，菱形眼，长尾上翘，分两缕向两侧舒卷，其上面上刻多道细密的刻线，利爪前蹬，赋予了力量感。

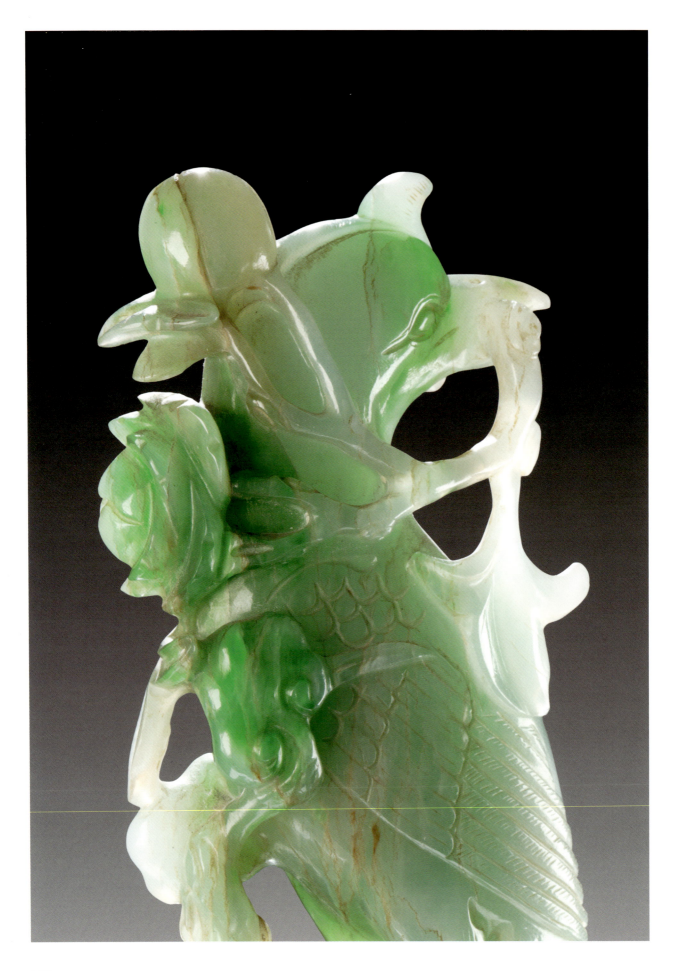

020 清　糯种阳绿凤穿牡丹（一对）

高190毫米　宽57毫米　厚25毫米

◆ 糯种，质地细腻，色泽莹润，局部带阳绿。圆雕双凤站于山石之上，呈回首相望状，嘴衔牡丹花卉，花瓣饱满，凤鸟身形矫健，羽翼收于腹部两侧，用阴刻线和网格纹雕琢出美丽的羽翅，四道凤尾自然下垂。

021 清 冰糯种双凤衔牡丹

高 71.4 毫米　长 100 毫米　厚 35 毫米

◆ 冰糯种，质地细腻，色泽莹润，水绿色。
圆雕双凤立于山石之上，一凤口衔牡丹花，取
凤穿牡丹之意，一凤昂首挺胸，双翅贴于两侧，
长尾卷曲支地，羽翼采用线刻的技法，精细
整齐。寓意荣华富贵。

021 清　冰糯种双凤衔牡丹

022 清 冰种飘绿凤衔牡丹

高 112 毫米　宽 56 毫米　厚 20 毫米

◆ 冰种，质地细腻，温润透亮，带阳绿。圆雕凤鸟站于山石之上，双目圆睁，凤冠微翘，嘴衔牡丹，花瓣饱满，枝叶舒卷，凤凰身姿优美，羽翼收于腹部两侧，凤尾自然下垂卷曲。"凤穿牡丹"寓意吉祥富贵。

023 清　糯种三色耄耋富贵

高 112 毫米　宽 90 毫米　厚 42 毫米

◆ 糯种，质地细腻，白、红、绿三色，色彩丰富。以圆雕和镂雕工艺雕琢，两只巧色蝴蝶和蝈蝈，挥展双翼，翩翩而来，色白处巧雕一蝈蝈，嘴衔折枝花卉；另一侧花叶中一猫，抬头仰望，尾巴高高翘起，细密的阴刻线雕琢出毛发，顽皮之姿尽显其中；画面动感十足，蝴蝶、灵猫、蝈蝈处于不同的空间层次中，立体感强。此器寓意富贵耄耋。

◆ 冰糯种，质地细腻，色泽莹润，黄翡巧色。圆雕一童子，身着宽袖长袍，流畅飘逸，童子左手放置于身前，右手执盒于头顶，盒为黄翡巧色，应为和合童子之一。

024 清　冰糯种黄翡巧色和合童子

高 96 毫米　宽 35 毫米　厚 21.5 毫米

◆ 冰糯种，质地细腻，色泽莹润，黄翡巧色。圆雕一童子，身着宽袖长袍，流畅飘逸，童子左手放置于身前，右手执盒于头顶，盒为黄翡巧色，应为和合童子之一。

025 清 冰糯种佛坐像

高 45.4 毫米　宽 37.2 毫米　厚 11.9 毫米

◆ 冰糯种，质地细腻，晶莹通透。圆雕坐佛，盘腿而坐于蒲团之上，脸型秀丽，螺髻高耸，大耳垂贴于面部两侧，面部慈祥，身着袒右肩式僧衣，两手放在腹部前面，作禅定印。

026 清　糯种二甲传胪

长 103 毫米　宽 72 毫米　厚 21 毫米

◆ 糯种，质地细腻，温润透亮，水绿色。圆雕两只螃蟹，蟹壳微隆，八足屈张各异，前螯张开聚拢，似要钳住蟹身下的芦叶、芦花，芦叶自由舒展。寓"二甲传胪"之意。

在古代科举考试中，殿试以后由第二甲第一名宣布登第进士名次的典礼，叫做"传胪"，即依次唱名。故玉雕中二蟹即意为"二甲"，其所穿行于芦花、芦叶之间即"穿芦"以谐音"传胪"。

027 清　糯种红翡巧色八方来财

高 17.4 毫米　宽 59.3 毫米　厚 36.8 毫米

◆ 糯种，质地细腻，色泽莹润，带红翡。螃蟹甲
壳红翡巧色，八爪蜷缩，圆睛凸起，蟹有八只脚，
寓意八方来财。

028 清　冰种飘绿八骏马（一组八件）

高 52 毫米　宽 36 毫米　厚 18 毫米

◆ 冰种，质地细腻，色泽莹润，飘绿花。以圆雕工艺雕琢出一幅八骏图，骏马膘肥体壮，四肢有力，双耳或直立，或后竖，马尾微卷，马鬃以阴刻线表现。动作姿态各异，或低头喝水，或回首凝视，或仰卧休憩，或挺胸抬头。

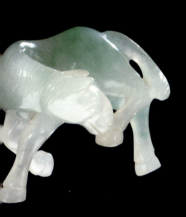

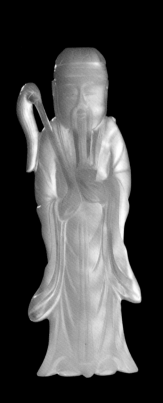

029 清 冰种飘蓝八仙

大 高 76.8 毫米 宽 23.8 毫米 厚 21 毫米
小 高 70 毫米 宽 28.3 毫米 厚 17.3 毫米（大小不一）

◆ 冰种，质地细腻，晶莹通透，局部飘蓝花。以圆雕工艺雕琢张
果老、吕洞宾、韩湘子、何仙姑、铁拐李、钟离全、曹国舅、蓝
采和八仙，身着宽袖长袍，衣褶线条婉转流畅，手执法器，发髻、
胡须采用细密阴刻线雕琢。人物神态动作刻画各异，形神俱备。

030 创汇期 糯种圆雕大象（一组四件）

大 高 52.7 毫米 宽 74 毫米 厚 27.3 毫米
小 高 45 毫米 宽 64.5 毫米 厚 27.7 毫米

◆ 糯种，质地细腻，色泽莹润。这组作品表现的是四只大小不一、体态肥硕的大象，它们神态动作生动有趣，大象四肢前屈，粗壮有力，鼻子或上扬，或卷鼻。

031 清　糯种红翡巧色刘海金蟾

高 85.5 毫米　宽 98 毫米　厚 41.6 毫米

◆ 糯种,质地细腻,色泽莹润。刘海仙,呈蹲坐状,眉眼开阔,身着宽袍广袖,腰扎细带,左手举握一镂空巧色铜钱,右手环抱红翡巧色金蟾,寓意财源茂盛,取之不竭。

032 清 糯种三色刘海金蟾

高 41 毫米　宽 50.7 毫米　厚 27.4 毫米

● 糯种，质地较为细腻。黄、白、绿三色，色彩丰富。此件刘海戏金蟾摆件采用圆雕技法雕琢刘海坐卧，丰颊宽颊，衣纹刻画简练，手执铜钱，戏逗金蟾，寓意洪福齐天。

033 清　冰糯种红翡巧色刘海金蟾

高 42.6 毫米　宽 58.5 毫米　厚 21.4 毫米

◆ 冰糯种，质地细腻，色泽莹润。此件圆雕摆件以红翡巧雕而成。刘海呈横卧状，丰颊宽颊，开口憨笑，坦胸露乳，衣纹刻画简练，红皮巧色金蟾匍匐于右肩之上，乖巧可爱，吐出红翡巧色的串串铜钱，代表着财源广进之意。

034 清 冰种刘海金蟾

高 80.5 毫米　宽 55 毫米　厚 17.5 毫米

◆ 冰种，质地细腻，温润透亮，以镂雕和圆雕工艺雕琢一童子，开脸以阴刻线勾出五官轮廓，以突出立体感，橄榄形眼，鼻子上窄下宽，呈蒜头鼻，嘴角上翘。上身着宽袖左衽短衣，系腰带，衣褶纹沟明显，线条流畅婉转。刘海双手挥动一根穿着铜钱的飘带戏逗金蟾，寓意财源茂盛，取之不竭。

035 清　冰糯种红翡巧色刘海金蟾

高 50 毫米　宽 56.8 毫米　厚 21.5 毫米

◆ 冰糯种，质地细腻，色泽莹润，红翡巧色。圆雕刘海盘腿而坐，开脸生动，面相饱满，笑容憨态可掬，红翡巧色三足小金蟾，吐出串串铜钱，寓意财源茂盛、取之不竭。

036 清 糯种红翡巧色走马上任

高74毫米 宽28毫米 厚31毫米

◆ 糯种，质地细腻，色泽莹润，红翡巧色。圆雕一童子站立石上，一手牵马、一手执令牌。童子面部严肃，身着对襟窄袖衫，紧裤腿，身旁骏马抬头昂扬，张目前视，嘴微张，竖耳向前作警听状。巧色红翡石、马与童子形成鲜明的对比，有走马上任之意。

037 清　冰种阳绿马上得令

高 50 毫米　宽 39 毫米　厚 23 毫米

◆ 冰种，质地细腻，晶莹通透，飘阳绿。以
镂雕和圆雕技法雕琢一束发男子，斜襟窄袖
长袍，一手牵马，一手持三角令旗。胯下骏
马呈蹲卧状，前足一跪一起，后足贴卧于腹下。
马回首凝望，似在随时接受指令。整件作品
寓意"马上得令"。

冰糯种，质地温润细腻。圆雕持莲童子，以阴线刻画五官，嘴上翘，目微闭，娇憨可爱，天真秀气。其寓意为连生贵子。

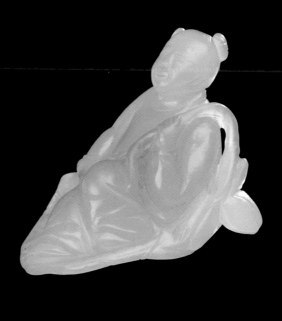

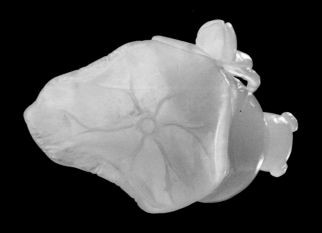

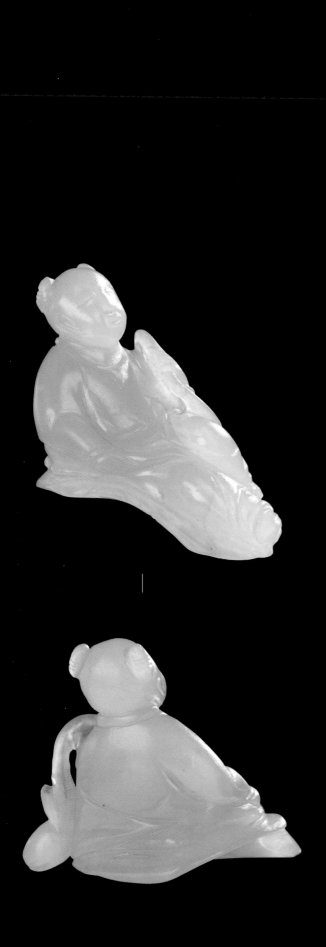

038 清　冰糯种连生贵子

高 46.5 毫米　宽 36.1 毫米　厚 41.3 毫米

◆ 冰糯种，质地温润细腻。圆雕持莲童子，以阴线刻画五官，嘴上翘，目微闭，娇憨可爱，天真秀气。其寓意为连生贵子。

039 清　糯种三色童子戏象

高 60 毫米　宽 62.6 毫米　厚 24.9 毫米

◆ 糯种，质地细腻，黄、绿、白三色，色彩丰富。象作行走状，长鼻后卷。一童子跪坐于象上正与其嬉戏，头部黄翡巧色。整器有"喜庆吉祥""太平有象"的美好寓意。

040 清　糯种红翡巧色五福童子

高 65.6 毫米　宽 39 毫米　厚 23 毫米

◆ 糯种，质地细腻，色泽莹润。以圆雕技法雕琢
引福童子，面带微笑，身着短衣，手捧宝瓶；童
子似作回首状，与红翡巧色蝙蝠相互呼应，体态
生动写实；身上衣褶柔美细腻，富有动感，寓意
佳美。

041 清　糯种阳绿伏虎罗汉

高 95 毫米　宽 50 毫米　厚 14 毫米

◆ 糯种，质地细腻，色泽莹润，飘阳绿，此
即俗称"白底青"。圆雕伏虎罗汉，怒目圆睁，
披僧袍，一手握镂雕金刚圈，一手紧握拳头。
右腿站立，左腿弯曲，画面中并未出现虎，却
给人造成伏虎状，匠心独运。罗汉本有驱妖
降魔之本领，此摆件亦有庇护平安之意。

042 清　糯种飘绿老少同乐

高 46.8 毫米　宽 69 毫米　厚 48 毫米

◆ 糯种，质地细腻，色泽莹润，飘绿。整件
作品惟妙惟肖，生动鲜活，孩子的天真可爱，
长须飘飘的长者惬意陶然，构成了一副生动立
体、抒发天伦之乐的图画。人物刻画细腻逼真，
琢工精致，线条流畅。

044 清　冰糯种红翡巧色东方朔偷桃

高 65 毫米　宽 83.6 毫米　厚 28.4 毫米

◆ 冰糯种，质地细腻，色泽莹润，红翡巧色。此作选取"东方朔偷桃"题材，采用圆雕手法刻画东方朔，天庭饱满，长须一垂到胸际，身着宽袍广袖，斜右倚山石，左手捧仙桃，身后红翡巧色雕蝙蝠、山石。汉武帝寿辰之日，西王母以仙桃五枚献与武帝，言：此桃三千年一生实。指东方朔言：他曾三次偷食我的仙桃。据此而有东方朔偷桃之说，东方朔以寿一万八千年而被奉为"寿星"，此题材也即经典的长寿吉祥寓意。

045 清　糯种红翡巧色太白醉酒

高 45.5 毫米　宽 49 毫米　厚 20.8 毫米

◆ 糯种，质地细腻，色泽莹润，红翡巧色。圆雕一文人蜷腿屈坐于仙槎之上，头戴学士巾，神态放松微醺，一手执酒杯倚放腿上；另一手自然垂下，身后一大坛酒。整个仙槎巧色红翡，两头翘起。这幅作品寓意太白醉酒，为文人案头雅玩。

046 清 糯种飘绿太白醉酒

高 42.4 毫米　宽 50.9 毫米　厚 39.7 毫米

◆ 糯种，质地细腻，浅绿色。圆雕太白醉酒坐像。头戴逍遥巾，身着广袖长衫，长髯飘飘，垂于胸前，醉意朦胧，左手拿一酒杯，右手自然垂落于右膝，缩于衣袖间执酒坛。"太白醉酒"为明清时玉雕中常见题材之一。

043 清　糯种阳绿南极仙翁

高 100 毫米　宽 38 毫米　厚 19 毫米

◆ 糯种，质地较为细腻，色泽莹润，飘阳绿。采用圆雕工艺雕刻了一"南极仙翁"像，仙翁高额隆起，圆润饱满，阴刻线髯须，身着长袍宽袖，左手拄拐，右手环抱巧色灵芝。

047 清 糯种三色巧雕福禄寿

长 62.7 毫米　宽 48.7 毫米　厚 32.8 毫米

◆ 糯种，质地细腻，色泽莹润，三色巧雕，色彩丰富。寿星为白须老翁，额部隆起，左手持龙首口衔如意拐杖，如意巧色，肩扛一巧色蝙蝠，寓意"福禄寿"。

048 清　糯种红翡巧色辈辈封侯

通高 62 毫米　宽 30.6 毫米　厚 24 毫米

◆ 糯种，质地较为细腻，色泽莹润，红翡巧色。圆雕灵猴二只，红翡巧色而成的幼猴伶俐乖巧，依偎于大猴背上，大猴蜷曲而坐，憨态可掬。整幅作品精雕细琢，巧妙运用巧色，线条自然流畅，神态刻画清晰明了。有"辈辈封侯"之意。

049 清　糯种阳绿马上封侯

高 52.4 毫米　宽 59.6 毫米　厚 19 毫米

◆ 糯种，质地较为细腻，色泽莹润，飘阳绿。骏马膘肥体健，四肢粗壮短小，与匍匐于马背上的猴子形成呼应之势，整体线条自然流畅。有"马上封侯"的传统吉祥寓意。

俗称"白底青"。圆雕一对狮子，两首相对。
鬃毛卷曲细顺，两只狮子双目圆瞪，欲张
口衔绣球绶带，绣球表面布满阴刻线纹。

050 清　糯种阳绿双狮戏球

高 54 毫米　宽 57 毫米　厚 25 毫米

◆ 糯种，质地细腻，色泽莹润，飘阳绿，
俗称"白底青"。圆雕一对狮子，两首相对。
鬃毛卷曲细顺，两只狮子双目圆瞪，欲张
口衔绣球绶带，绣球表面布满阴刻线纹。

051 清 糯种飘绿瑞兽

高 63.8 毫米　宽 124.2 毫米　厚 51 毫米

◆ 糯种，质地细腻，色泽莹润，飘绿。瑞兽双目圆睁，口衔灵芝，四肢卧于地，兽尾扬起，正折身回首，神情严肃。瑞兽衔芝，寓意长寿吉祥。

052 清　冰糯种三色风云际会（一对）

左　高113毫米　宽88毫米　厚18毫米
右　高109毫米　宽82毫米　厚27毫米

◆ 冰糯种，质地细腻，色泽莹润，黄、绿、紫三色，色彩丰富。圆雕两只猛虎立于山石之侧，昂首挺胸，尾巴翘起，呈蓄势待发状。两只黄翡巧色双龙脚踏祥云，立于石上，昂首对望，气势威猛，呈优美的 S 形，双龙嘴衔绶带，左边中空阳绿巧色镂雕宝珠，实为点睛之笔。寓意"风云际会"。

053 清　糯种三色双狮

长 95 毫米　厚 36 毫米　高 52 毫米

◆ 糯种，质地较为细腻，色泽莹润，红、绿、白三色。以圆雕手法雕刻一狮子，体型健硕，两眼圆睁，极有气势，在狮子前面卧着一红翡巧色小狮子，灵动活泼。背部、两侧、尾部雕琢平行的阴线细纹以示毛髪。狮子有瑞兽之誉，二狮相戏，谐称"太师少师"古三公中位最尊者为"太师"，"少师"与"少傅"，"少保"合称"三少"。以"狮""师"同音，以"太师少师"为高位的象征，而借音借意以狮为师是官运亨通之意。

054 清 冰糯种象

高 28 毫米　宽 36.7 毫米　厚 19.4 毫米

◆ 冰糯种,质地细腻,色泽莹润,微带紫色。象呈跪卧状,鼻卷牙伸,尾上翘贴于身上,以简单的阴刻线勾勒出躯体四肢、简练而有力。

055 清 糯种饕餮纹如意

长 350 毫米　宽 78.4 毫米　厚 36.7 毫米

◆ 糯种，质地细腻。柄身呈 S 型，弧度优美，如意首为灵芝形，由卷云纹和饕餮纹组成，柄身布满卷云纹，柄尾饰饕餮纹，为浅浮雕工艺。此件为典型清代中期宫廷玉器。

056 清　红木嵌翡翠如意

通长310毫米　如意头长86毫米　宽68毫米　厚18毫米

◆ 糯种，质地较为细腻，色泽莹润，飘蓝花。如意的造型，是由
云纹、灵芝做成头部，然后衔接一长柄而成。柄身为红木，柄首
做成如意形，浮雕佛手、寿桃及枝繁叶茂的花卉。

057 清　糯种飘绿三多九如福寿如意

长 396 毫米　宽 86.8 毫米　高 52.7 毫米

◆ 糯种，质地细腻，色泽莹润，飘绿花。以圆雕、浮雕、镂雕工艺雕琢而成，柄身呈 S 型，弧度优美，如意首为灵芝形，上饰桃实，一蝙蝠伏卧于桃枝上，柄身以镂雕和浮雕工艺布满桃枝，延伸到柄尾，柄尾雕一蝙蝠，与柄首蝙蝠遥相呼应，九个桃实饱满丰硕，枝叶自由舒展。

058 清　冰种飘蓝暗八仙五蝠捧寿如意

长 394 毫米　宽 84.8 毫米　高 54.2 毫米

◆ 冰种，质地细腻，色泽莹润，飘蓝花。以圆雕、浮雕工艺雕琢而成，柄首边沿一圈回纹，中间由五只蝙蝠围着寿字构成，寓意多福多寿。柄身一周回纹，表面浮雕暗八仙纹，有葫芦、扇子、鱼鼓、宝剑、荷花、花篮、横笛和阴阳板等。暗八仙纹饰是一种由八仙纹派生而来的宗教纹样，此种纹样中并不出现人物，而是以道教中八仙各自的法器代表各位神仙，蝙蝠之蝠与福字同音，故以五蝠代表五福，五蝠常常围一寿字，俗称"五蝠捧寿"。

059 清　糯种双龙首钟

直径 103 毫米　高 94 毫米

◆ 糯种，温润细腻，色泽莹润。钟型，钟体轮廓外敞平滑，钟口外圈为周饰回纹，钟身布满绳结纹，钟顶部雕双龙首形钮，龙首相对，张口，圆眼涡鼻，双耳紧贴颈部。

060 清 红木座糯种飘绿海屋添筹图插屏

高 240 毫米　宽 150 毫米　厚 9.9 毫米

◆ 糯种，质地细腻，色泽莹润，飘绿带紫。插屏为双面雕工，
面所雕波澜壮阔的海水，灵芝，楼阁凌驾在云朵之上，仙鹤嘴里衔
筹翩飞而至；另一面瑞鹤、仙鹿、牡丹等，皆刻画细致。此为"海
屋添筹"题材，寓意吉祥长寿。

061 清　红木嵌翠福寿如意插屏

通高 400 毫米　宽 320 毫米
瓦子长 108 毫米　宽 97 毫米

◆ 糯种，质地细腻，色泽莹润。插屏采用红木镂雕缠枝花卉纹饰而成，中间镶嵌一浮雕翡翠瓦子，中间雕琢有两个寿桃，一蝙蝠飞舞，栩栩如生。整件插屏代表吉祥如意，福寿平安。

062 清　红木座嵌冰糯种英雄斗志插屏

高 130 毫米　宽 134 毫米

◆ 冰糯种，质地细腻，色泽莹润，通体黄翡。插屏采用红木镂雕而成，屏风中间镶嵌一长方形浅浮雕屏芯，画面中以减地浮雕工艺雕琢太阳、祥云、常青松柏、兰花，一鹰站于山石上，低头回首，似栖息状，一两尾瑞兽呈伏卧状，双耳直立，回首凝望。

063 清　红木座糯种三色童子拜观音插屏

长 72.8 毫米　宽 65 毫米　厚 9 毫米

◆ 糯种，质地细腻，黄、绿、白三色巧雕。底座为红木如意纹镂雕工艺。插屏采用双面浮雕工艺，一面浅浮雕一尊坐式翡翠观音，头戴宝冠，身着宽袖长袍、闭眼遐思、合手端坐，童子纯真可爱，绶带环绕，呈拜服菩萨状，虔诚质朴。观音身后满饰花卉以及各种题材的图案符号。另一面与其遥相呼应，雕刻有仙台楼阁，梅花鹿仰头望仙鹤。

064 清　红木框糯种群仙祝寿图插屏

宽 390 毫米　高 416 毫米　厚 13 毫米

◆ 糯种，质地细腻，色泽莹润，淡绿色带黄翡。屏心以浅浮雕工艺雕琢群仙祝寿图，亭台楼阁，树木繁茂，一棵棵松苍郁郁，枝干横卧上曲，松枝上长满一团团的松针，寿石突起，各种水仙花卉花叶自由舒展。亭台之上仙人姿态各异，寿星身着广袖长袍，右手持如意灵芝，童子扶持于侧，其余仙人也手持各色祝寿之物。亭台之下雕琢和合二仙，一童子骑仙鹿，手捧寿桃，另一童子手捧宝盒脚踏如意祥云纹而来，空中仙鹤展翅盘旋。此件为清代宫廷典型工艺。

065 清　糯种勾云纹磬

高 90.6 毫米　宽 172 毫米　厚 7 毫米

◆　糯种，质地细腻，淡绿色。磬为蝙蝠形，
通体饰勾云纹，琢制精细，为典型清中期
宫廷玉器风格。

066 清 糯种阳绿诗文插屏芯

长 87.8 毫米　宽 70.5 毫米　厚 3.2 毫米

◆ 糯种，质地细腻，色泽莹润，局部飘阳绿。插屏芯呈椭圆形，一面素面无纹，一面琢刻乾隆御制诗《题邹一桂写生卷九首·其三·长生花》：瑶池桃实三千岁，树各春秋不相妨。月月花开十二度，女夷批判岂辞忙。

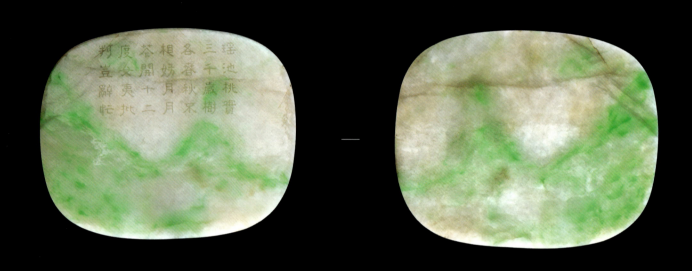

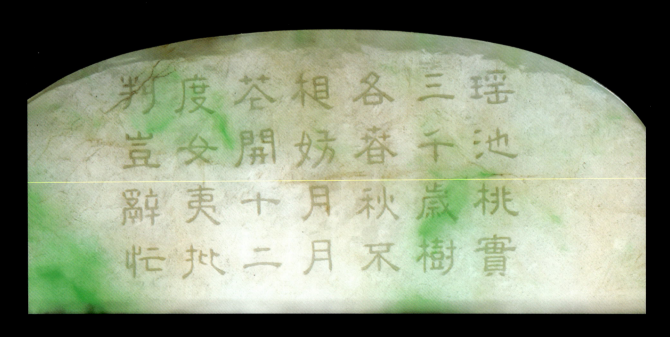

067 创汇期 糯种红翡巧色刘海金蟾

高 76 毫米 宽 90 毫米 厚 31 毫米

◆ 糯种，质地细腻，色泽莹润，红翡巧雕。以圆雕和镂雕的工艺刻画了刘海笑容可掬，一群红翡巧色蝙蝠伴随左右，衔绶带并串铜钱两枚，喻"福在眼前"。

器皿

间浅浮雕宝相花纹，四周环绕如意云头纹和缠
枝莲纹。寓意吉祥。

068 清　冰种飘黄宝相花盖盒

高 22 毫米　直径 29 毫米

◆ 冰种，莹润似水，青绿色，飘黄翡。整只
盖盒分上下两部分，天地盖，子母口。盒身扁圆，
腹部较深，顶部呈弧形，底部有圈足。盒盖中
间浅浮雕宝相花纹，四周环绕如意云头纹和缠
枝莲纹。寓意吉祥。

069 清　糯种飘绿盖盒

高 28 毫米　直径 51.4 毫米

◆　糯种，质地细腻，局部飘绿。整只盖盒分为盒身和盒盖上下两部分，天地盖，子母口，底部有圈足，腹部呈弧形，盒盖扁圆形，整器光素无纹。

070 清　冰糯种螭龙纹盖盒

长 64.6 毫米　宽 41 毫米　高 36.7 毫米

◆　冰糯种，温润细腻，淡绿色带黄翡。椭圆形，盖盒分上下两部分，顶部略扁平，圆口，腹部鼓出，下腹束收至底，圈足。盒盖上饰螭龙纹，以一首尾相接的龙盘绕，肩部两侧各饰一如意辅首衔环。盒盖浮雕上下口沿各雕琢一圈回纹，相互呼应。

071 清 冰糯种三阳开泰盖盒

高 56 毫米　直径 78.3 毫米

◆ 冰糯种，质地细腻。盒身圆，子母口，斜腹，底有圈足。盒盖正中高浮雕宝相花，盒盖外圈浮雕三只呈伏卧状羊，身躯饱满肥硕，头部较小，呈三角形，背部丰满，短颈，昂首目视前方。寓意"三阳开泰"。

072 清　紫檀盖冰种盖盒

高 33.5 毫米　直径 59.2 毫米

◆ 冰种，晶莹通透。整只盖盒分上下两部
分，天地盖，子母口。盒身为圆形，盒盖
扁平，为紫檀做成。整器光素无纹。

073 清　糯种阳绿花开富贵盖盒

长 100.5 毫米　高 78 毫米　厚 38 毫米

◆ 糯种，质地细腻，飘阳绿，俗称"白底青"。该盒为扁圆形，
分盖和盒身两部分，盖钮为环状，套两环。其两侧竖狮首双耳衔环，
盖和盒身布满浅浮雕牡丹花卉纹，椭圆形圈足，足外撇。

074 清　冰糯种宝相花盖盒

高 36.4 毫米　直径 71.7 毫米

◆ 冰糯种，玉质细腻，莹润有光泽，浅绿色。
圆柱形体，分盒盖和盒体两部分，子母口，盒
盖中央浮雕一枝宝相花，周围缠枝花卉纹环
绕。盒体光素无纹。

075 清 糯种双蝠捧寿盖盒

高 48.9 毫米　直径 51.9 毫米

◆ 糯种，质地细腻。圆柱体，分盒盖和盒身
两部分，子母口，盒盖表面为圆形，盖沿和
外圈周饰回纹，中间浅浮雕双蝠捧寿。盒体
腹部雕花卉，平底，底周饰回纹，和口沿处
互相呼应，形成一体。

076 清　冰种飘蓝暗八仙纹碗

高 54.7 毫米　直径 116 毫米

◆ 冰种，质地细腻，色泽通透，飘蓝花。碗身造型优美，敞口，近底渐收，厚圈足。外壁口沿、腹底各周饰回纹，腹部浮雕暗八仙纹。暗八仙纹是由八仙纹派生而来的宗教纹样，以道教中八仙各自所持之扇子、阴阳板、花篮、笛子、荷花等法器代表各位神仙。

077 清　冰种福寿三多纹碗（一对）

高 55 毫米　直径 110.8 毫米

◆ 冰种，质地温润细腻，晶莹通透。器形规整，圆口，口外撇，圈足，足外撇。口沿和碗底周饰回纹，以浅浮雕技法雕琢三多纹，佛手形态逼真写实，石榴饱满圆润，蝙蝠依附于其间，寓意福寿三多。

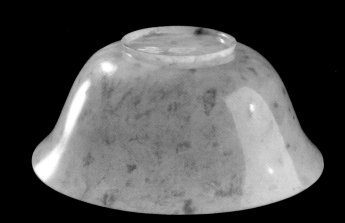

078 清　冰种飘蓝撇口碗

高 70 毫米　直径 183 毫米

◆ 冰种，晶莹通透，飘蓝花。器形规整，
圆口，口外撇，小圈足，足外撇。

079 清　糯种飘绿盖碗

通高 91.1 毫米　直径 113.5 毫米

◆　糯种，玉质细腻，飘浅绿。盖径小
于碗径，盖内扣于碗，圆形，撇口，圈足。
盖及碗皆光素。

080 清　冰糯种飘蓝撇口碗

高 60 毫米　直径 136.8 毫米

◆ 冰糯种，质地温润细腻，飘蓝花。碗身造型端庄，圆口，外撇，圈足。

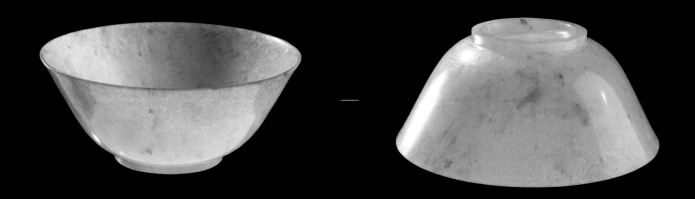

081 清 冰种撇口碗

高58毫米 直径116毫米

◆ 冰种，质地紧密且细腻，器形规整，圆
口，小圈足。

082 清　冰种碗

高 51 毫米　直径 109.8 毫米

◆ 冰种，质地细腻，色泽莹润，微带紫色。
器形较为规整，圆口，小圈足。

083 清　冰种碗

高 67 毫米　直径 105 毫米

◆ 冰种，玉质细腻，晶莹通透。器形规整，
圆口，小圈足。

084 清　冰种飘黄碗

高 60 毫米　直径 109 毫米

◆ 冰种，玉质细腻，轻薄通透，局部飘黄
翡。器形规整，圆口，碗壁弧内收，圈足。

085 清　冰种飘蓝碗

高 74 毫米　直径 137 毫米

◆ 冰种，玉质细腻，轻薄通透，带紫色，
飘蓝花。器形规整，圆口，口外撇，碗壁
弧内收，圈足，足外撇。

◆ 冰种，晶莹剔透，器形规整，圆口，口
沿平，碗壁弧内收，圈足，足外撇。

086 清　冰种碗

高 60 毫米　直径 160 毫米

◆ 冰种，晶莹剔透，器形规整，圆口，口
沿平，碗壁弧内收，圈足，足外撇。

087 清　豆种飘绿撇口起沿碗

高 65.4 毫米　直径 144 毫米

◆　豆种，颗粒较粗，此即典型老坑豆种，薄如
蝉翼，淡绿色。碗造型周正，薄胎，敞口，口
沿处起线，腹近底渐收，宽圈足。碗底中部刻
有"乾隆年制"篆书双行寄托款。

088 清 冰种三色牡丹纹盖碗

高 75 毫米　直径 116 毫米

◆ 冰种，质地细腻，色泽莹润，黄、绿、白三色，色彩丰富。盖径小于碗径，盖内扣于碗，圆形，敞口，圈足。盖及碗身皆满饰折枝牡丹纹，以细阴刻线表现纹路和叶脉，网格纹点缀花蕊。

089 清 冰种飘绿盖碗（一对）

高 45 毫米　直径 101 毫米

◆ 冰种，质地细腻，色泽莹润，飘绿花，晶
莹通透。盖内扣于碗，圆形，敞口，圈足。

090 清　冰种痕都斯坦风格菊瓣纹碗 (一对)

高 53 毫米　直径 140 毫米

◆ 冰种，质地细腻，色泽莹润，轻薄通透。圆形侈口，浅腹，圈足。通体菊瓣纹饰，为典型的痕都斯坦玉器风格。碗壁磨制精到，抛光细腻，造型柔美而不失规矩，显现一种温润、内敛的质感。

091 清　冰种飘蓝酒杯（二只）

大　高 25 毫米　直径 49.5 毫米
小　高 24.5 毫米　直径 41.2 毫米

◆ 冰种，温润剔透，飘蓝花。斗笠形，敞口，
斜壁，小圈足。

092 清　冰种飘蓝八棱酒杯（一对）

高 38.5 毫米　直径 49.8 毫米

◆ 冰种，晶莹通透，飘蓝花。杯体为八棱形，平口，小圈足。

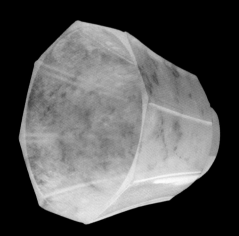

093 清　冰种八棱酒杯

高 34.7 毫米　直径 45.6 毫米

◆ 冰种，玉质细腻，轻薄通透。杯口圆形，杯体呈八棱状，实心圈足，圈心内凹。

高 42.2 毫米　直径 51.5 毫米

◆ 冰种，晶莹通透，飘蓝花。器身八棱状，足底内凹。

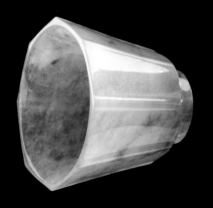

094 清　冰种飘蓝八棱酒杯（一对）

高 42.2 毫米　直径 51.5 毫米

◆ 冰种，晶莹通透，飘蓝花。器身八棱状，足底内凹。

095 清 糯种酒杯（一对）

高 26.4 毫米　直径 34.2 毫米

◆ 糯种，玉质细腻，色白如凝脂。圆口，口
外撇，腹下敛收，圈足。

◆ 冰糯种，质地细腻，飘蓝花。圆口，腹为
弧形束收至杯底，小圈足外撇。

096 清 冰糯种飘蓝花酒杯

高 36 毫米 直径 48.4 毫米

◆ 冰糯种，质地细腻，飘蓝花。圆口，腹为
弧形束收至杯底，小圈足外撇。

浮雕工艺，环绕杯体雕琢出枝蔓的婀娜多姿，两片树叶在杯体腹部舒展开来，以阴线刻雕琢出叶子的筋脉。

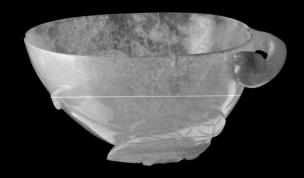

097 清　冰种秋叶杯

长 74.5 毫米　宽 58.5 毫米　高 35.3 毫米

◆ 冰种，质地细腻，晶莹通透。以镂雕和高浮雕工艺，环绕杯体雕琢出枝蔓的婀娜多姿，两片树叶在杯体腹部舒展开来，以阴线刻雕琢出叶子的筋脉。

098 清 冰糯种黄翡巧色松鼠葡萄杯

长 80 毫米　宽 56 毫米　高 31 毫米

◆ 冰糯种，质地细腻。以葡萄枝蔓为耳，浮雕出卷曲藤叶，巧色黄翡葡萄果实圆润，左边杯体高浮雕一巧色黄翡松鼠，趴卧于杯，呈回首状。

099 清 糯种黄翡巧色石榴杯

高 36.1 毫米　宽 73 毫米　厚 59 毫米

◆ 糯种，质地细腻，色泽莹润。杯体随形雕琢成石榴形，杯口呈石榴形，杯体高浮雕缠枝花卉纹，以双阴刻线雕琢出叶子的筋脉和纹路，清晰可见，杯口黄翡巧色。

100 清　糯种黄翡巧色佛手杯

高 32.6 毫米　长 76 毫米　厚 48.5 毫米

◆ 糯种，质地细腻。杯体随形雕琢成佛手形，杯口呈椭圆形。以高浮雕工艺雕琢出缠枝纹，叶片、枝蔓筋脉清晰可见，枝蔓根部及杯口黄翡巧色。

101 清 冰种飘蓝勾云纹团寿双耳杯

高 54.1 毫米 直径 81.4 毫米

◆ 冰种，质地细腻，清澈透亮，飘蓝花。圆口，腹下敛收，圈足。
镂空透雕寿字纹双耳，口沿和下腹部周饰回纹，腹部浅浮雕团寿，
勾云纹环绕。

102 清　糯种斗形福寿双耳杯（一对）

长 72.7 毫米　宽 51.1 毫米　高 42.7 毫米

◆ 糯种，温润细腻，有如凝脂。四方耳杯，杯体呈方口斗形，器型规整，敞口，杯口和杯底各环绕周饰回纹，杯身两侧镂雕三对卷云纹耳。

103 清　冰种三色瓜棱形双耳杯（一对）

高 53 毫米　直径 104 毫米

◆ 冰种，质地细腻，晶莹通透，红、黄、绿三色，色彩丰富多样。
呈六瓣瓜棱形，花形口，腹为弧形，束收至杯底，S 形双耳，花
形圈足外撇。

104 清 冰种痕都斯坦风格双耳杯

长 72 毫米　宽 44 毫米　高 59 毫米

◆ 冰种，质地细腻，色泽莹润，带有斑点状黄翡与绿翠。器形为长方杯形，侈口收腹，高足微斜，器壁极薄，打磨极精。近口沿处周饰卷尾变体蕉叶纹，腹及足为莲瓣，双耳为两片叶片相夹的海棠花，琢工精湛。杯整体仿痕都斯坦玉器风格，工精器美，为典型清代宫廷玉器。

105 清　冰糯种桃形杯（一对）

长 80 毫米　宽 71 毫米　高 35 毫米

◆　冰糯种，质地细腻，色泽莹润，飘绿。口呈桃形，深腹，以镂
雕和浮雕工艺雕琢折枝花卉，以根茎成耳，茎叶延伸到杯底，叶
开两枝，自由舒展，以双阴刻线表现叶子的筋脉，雕琢精致。

◆ 冰种，质地细腻，晶莹通透，红、绿、白三色。杯敞口，斜壁，圈足。盏托为海棠形。

106 清　冰种三色杯盏（一对）

托长 81 毫米　宽 74 毫米　高 26 毫米
杯高 49.5 毫米　直径 67.2 毫米

◆ 冰种，质地细腻，晶莹通透，红、绿、白三色。杯敞口，斜壁，圈足。盏托为海棠形。

107 清 冰种飘蓝海棠形盏托（一对）

长 102.1 毫米　宽 84.5 毫米　高 11.5 毫米

◆ 冰种，质地细腻，通透轻薄，飘蓝花。器型为海棠形，中间设
圆形台，一周凸起，为放盏之用。底部矮圈足为海棠形。

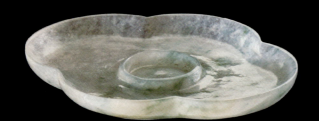 

108 清 糯种圆盘（一对）

高 27 毫米　直径 145 毫米

◆　糯种，质地较为细腻。圆形盘状，敞口，矮圈足。

109 清 冰种撇口起沿盘

高 33 毫米 直径 154 毫米

◆ 冰种，质地细腻，晶莹通透。圆口，外撇
起沿，浅腹，平底，圈足。

110 清　冰种飘蓝花盘（一对）

高 24.3 毫米　直径 152 毫米

◆ 冰种，质地细腻莹润，飘蓝花。圆形盘状，敞口，口沿起线，平底，矮圈足。

111 清　冰种痕都斯坦风格海棠形菊瓣纹赏盘（一对）

长 150 毫米　宽 88 毫米　高 32 毫米

◆ 冰种，质地细腻，晶莹透彻。呈海棠形，平底、薄圈足。中间以网格纹作花蕊，向外
有三层花瓣，第二层花瓣卷曲呈圈足，第三层弯曲向上，成为既细又薄的弧形盘壁，延
伸到口沿。胎体透薄，玻璃质感强烈，为典型的痕都斯坦风格。

112 清 糯种长方水仙盆（一对）

长 145 毫米　宽 107 毫米　高 57 毫米

◆ 糯种，质地细腻，为同料所制，微带紫色。器形为无孔水仙盆，长方形，斜壁，器壁极薄；口有出沿，沿上浅浮雕缠枝莲；四足内收。整体器形工整流畅，韵致清雅。

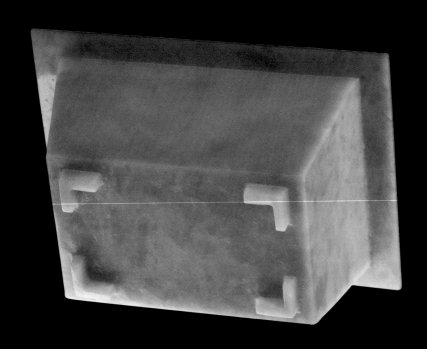

113 清　冰糯种飘绿宝相花小赏瓶

高 60 毫米　宽 30 毫米　厚 20.5 毫米

◆ 冰糯种，质地细腻，飘绿。椭圆形，分上下两部分，覆斗形盖，盖钮为椭圆形。直颈，弧腹，圈足。肩出双耳衔环，口沿周饰回纹，瓶腹两边均浅浮雕宝相花，四周环绕如意云头纹。

114 清　冰糯种飘蓝丹凤朝阳小赏瓶

高 82.4 毫米　直径 34 毫米

◆ 冰糯种,质地细腻,飘蓝花。撇口,长颈,溜肩,圆腹,腹下渐收,圈足略高,口部一道阴刻线,颈部一周蕉叶纹,腹部丹凤朝阳纹。

115 清 糯种红翡巧色喜上眉梢花插

带座高 168.9 毫米　宽 85.2 毫米　厚 57.9 毫米

◆ 糯种，温润细腻。整体造型呈梅桩形，周身以高浮雕和镂雕工艺雕琢梅枝，枝叶横斜，梅花瓣瓣铺展，红翡巧色一枝梅，两只喜鹊立于枝头，呈回首凝视状。

116 清　糯种黄翡巧色梅桩花插

高 190 毫米　宽 48.4 毫米　厚 33.5 毫米

◆ 糯种，质地细腻，色泽莹润，黄翡巧色。内部深掏膛，厚壁，口沿随形而饰，外壁为高浮雕梅花，枝干虬曲。

117 清　糯种飘绿西番莲纹莲瓣底座赏瓶

高 230 毫米　直径 39.8 毫米

◆ 糯种，质地细腻，带绿，俗称"白底青"。敞口，束颈，直腹下收，瓶身减地满浮雕缠枝西番莲纹，枝蔓舒展自如，底足周饰变体莲纹。带连体底座，底座装饰成莲花瓣状。

◆ 糯种，质地细腻，淡青色。为六棱形，
镂空兽耳。

118 清 糯种兽耳六棱赏瓶

高 170 毫米　宽 78.3 毫米　厚 39.6 毫米

◆ 糯种，质地细腻，淡青色。为六棱形，
镂空兽耳。

119 清　糯种牡丹纹四方双耳赏瓶

高 225 毫米　宽 71.2 毫米　厚 46.5 毫米

◆　糯种，质地细腻，浅绿，局部飘黄翡。此瓶四方口，束颈，腹部略呈弧形，底足外撇，口平直，四角雕琢四只蝙蝠，口沿、足、四边周饰回纹。颈部镂空耳，上饰蝙蝠和回纹，瓶身浅浮雕牡丹花卉纹。

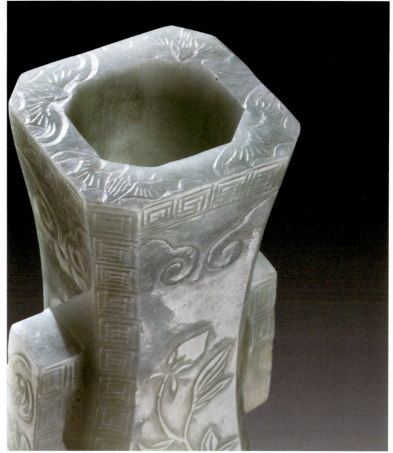

120 清　糯种紫罗兰饕餮纹花觚（一对）

高 160 毫米　宽 74.1 毫米　厚 41.9 毫米

◆ 糯种，质地细腻，通体浅紫色。方口，口沿与底部周饰回纹，腹部四面以浅浮雕工艺饰饕餮兽面纹，花觚上下四面各饰镂空耳，下衔活环。

121 清 糯种喜鹊登梅大赏瓶

高 250 毫米　宽 190 毫米　厚 82 毫米

◆ 糯种，玉质细腻，深绿色。瓶圆口，束颈，圆肩，腹下敛收，平底。肩出双如意耳，耳下衔环。通体以高浮雕和镂雕技法雕花鸟纹，一树梅花上下两只喜鹊，几丛菊花，阴刻线雕琢出枝叶的筋脉，卷云纹勾出菊花盛开的花瓣，构图雅致。菊花、喜鹊登梅意寓吉祥如意。

122 清　糯种嵌阳绿凤穿牡丹纹象耳衔环扁瓶

高 242 毫米　宽 110 毫米　厚 51.8 毫米

◆　糯种，质地较为细腻，飘阳绿。瓶扁平状，方口，束颈，口沿和盖
沿周饰回纹。象耳，衔环。颈上雕刻勾云纹。圆腹上两边浅浮雕凤鸟、
牡丹纹，为"凤穿牡丹"。盖上雕龙纹和勾云纹，龙双目圆睁，张牙舞爪，
龙身蜿蜒盘旋，宝珠钮。耳、环及瓶身阳绿花卉为嵌接镶嵌，镶嵌处
以榫卯插嵌，此为晚清时一种翡翠摆件制作的传统工艺，相对罕见。

123 清 冰种黄翡巧色双龙赏瓶

高 153 毫米 宽 98 毫米 厚 66 毫米

◆ 冰种，玉质细腻，晶莹通透。赏瓶分盖和瓶体两部分，龙抱宝珠钮，椭圆形口，束颈，美人肩，圈足。盖上以镂雕和高浮雕工艺雕琢一黄翡巧色龙呈蜿蜓盘旋状，环抱一珠。一侧以镂空雕刻的技法雕琢一折枝带叶的佛手，小鸟站立其上，呈侧回首状。另一侧以镂雕和高浮雕工艺雕琢一飞龙，龙为黄翡巧色，龙身呈 S 状，其间环绕灵芝。

124 清　糯种龙纹双耳壁瓶

带座高 215 毫米　宽 74.5 毫米　厚 32.8 毫米

◆ 糯种，质地较为细腻，泛浅绿色。壁瓶
形状宛如剖开的半个花瓶，靠墙的一面平
直，有连背式底座。整器敞口，平唇，瓶
口呈弓形，长颈，鼓腹，圈足。颈处出两耳，
镂雕成龙纹。瓶身浅浮雕花卉纹，云头如
意纹，龙纹。

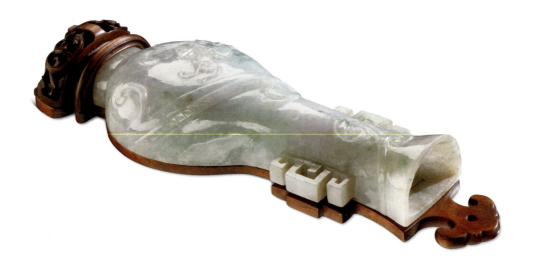

125 清　冰糯种炉瓶盒三事

炉　高 78.5 毫米　宽 77.7 毫米　厚 38.4 毫米
瓶　高 78.6 毫米　宽 32.2 毫米　厚 13.6 毫米
盒　高 46 毫米　宽 33.8 毫米　厚 20 毫米

◆　冰糯种，玉质细腻，色泽莹润，淡绿色。炉为鼓腹带盖，宝莲花盖钮，腹部两侧镂雕龙耳衔环，下承三兽足。炉体浮雕兽面纹及宝莲花纹，盖缘、炉口各周饰回纹。

瓶为扁平式，直口带盖，颈部略收、溜肩、弧腹下收至足，圈足外撇，口、足均为椭圆形。肩部兽耳衔环，颈部周饰蕉叶纹，腹部宝莲花纹，盖缘、瓶口及底足外沿均周饰回纹。

盒呈扁圆形，子母口，椭圆形口、足。覆斗形器盖，盖钮圆雕一狻猊，盖缘、瓶口及底足外沿均周饰回纹。炉、瓶、盒常在一起搭配，三件一组被称为"三事"。

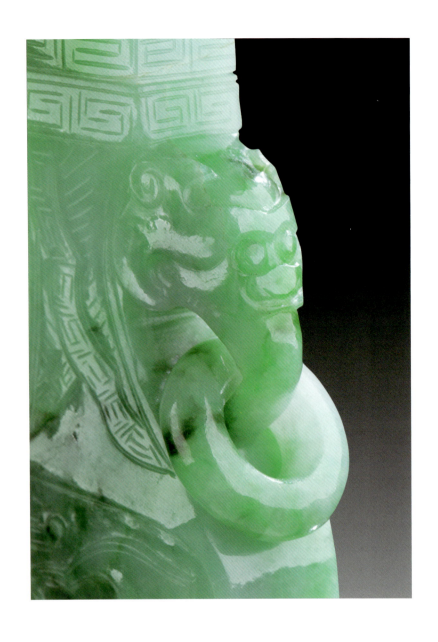

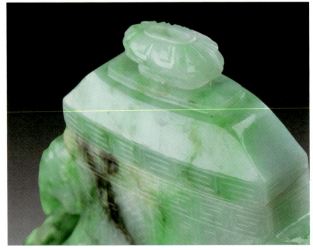

126 清　糯种阳绿饕餮纹象耳衔环扁瓶

高 180 毫米　宽 106.4 毫米　厚 29.7 毫米

◆ 糯种，质地细腻，飘阳绿。瓶体略扁，直口带盖，颈部略收，溜肩，弧腹，圈足略外撇。覆斗形器盖，莲花式宝珠钮，盖缘、瓶口各周饰回纹，颈部两侧出象耳衔环，颈部一周饰蕉叶纹。器腹主体为饕餮纹，周饰如意云纹。

127 民国　糯种紫罗兰牧牛图狮钮龙耳衔环扁瓶

高 340 毫米　宽 130 毫米　厚 57 毫米

◆ 糯种，质地细腻，色泽莹润，通体淡紫色。瓶盖为覆斗形，上饰立狮钮，盖及瓶口周饰回纹。瓶方口，溜肩，出双龙耳衔环，正背高浮雕狮首，腹正背饰牧童骑牛放纸鸢，瓶侧饰蝠磬双鱼，束收足，正背有狮首衔环。

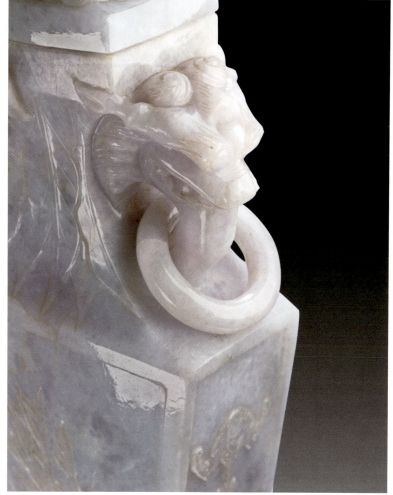

128 清　冰种岁岁平安小赏瓶

高 127 毫米　腹径 48 毫米

◆ 冰种，质地细腻，温润通透，通体水绿色。直口带盖，覆钵式盖，宝莲花钮，腹扁圆，束颈，弧腹内收至足，足外撇。颈部雕琢折枝花卉纹，腹颈连接处周饰如意纹，腹部满工锦地纹，瓶腹浅浮雕两株麦穗和两只鹌鹑。此瓶掏膛极薄,工艺精湛。寓意"岁岁平安"。

129 清　冰种饕餮纹双龙耳衔环赏瓶

高147毫米　宽114毫米　厚68毫米

◆ 冰种，质地细腻晶莹通透。盖为椭圆形，盖上衔环，桃形钮。
直口，折肩，肩出双龙耳衔环，腹部一周浮雕饕餮纹。腹内收至底，
椭圆形圈足，足外撇。器型端庄大气，工艺精湛。

130 清　冰种高浮雕三螭提链赏瓶

高 77.2 毫米　宽 60 毫米　厚 29.3 毫米

↴　冰种，质地细腻，晶莹通透。器分盖与瓶两部分，以镂雕提链相连，直口，束颈，折肩，腹下收至底，圈足外撇。赏瓶椭圆形盖，盖上高浮雕螭龙钮，肩出一耳下衔提链，腹部高浮雕火焰，中有圆珠，下方一龙向下俯冲，另一龙卷曲朝上，龙首相对。

131 清 糯种三色高浮雕鹭鸶荷叶赏瓶（一对）

高 150 毫米　宽 77 毫米　厚 20.9 毫米

◆ 糯种，质地细腻，红、绿、白三色。器分盖与瓶两部分，直口，束颈，折肩，腹下收至底，圈足外撇。椭圆形覆斗式盖，高浮雕鹭鸶荷叶为盖钮，腹部浮雕折枝莲叶、莲花，肩部出两耳，一侧红翡巧色镂雕莲枝莲叶，两只鹭鸶位于瓶下腹部两侧，回首对望。

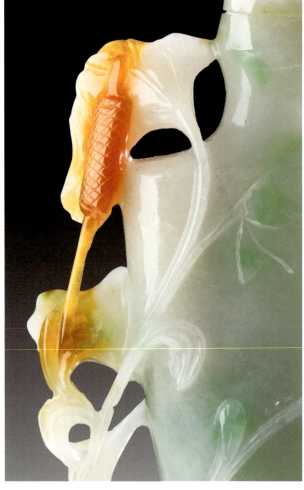

259

132 清　糯种阳绿巧色天鸡尊

高 210 毫米　长 190 毫米　厚 47 毫米

◆　糯种，质地细腻，温润透亮，阳绿巧色，色彩艳丽。运用了镂空、透雕、圆雕多种工艺手段雕琢而成天鸡尊的造型，天鸡直立，回首而望，双翅贴体，雕琢如意纹，长尾卷曲支地，双爪有力。背负一尊瓶，敞口，束颈，扁圆腹，尊身雕一对螭龙，一龙盘旋于肩部，另一龙昂首立于鸡身，双龙嘴衔折枝桃实。

133 清　冰种三色绳纹龙钮双螭耳扁瓶

高129毫米　宽128毫米　厚37.3毫米

● 冰种，质地细腻，色泽莹润，晶莹通透，黄、绿、白三色，色彩丰富。器分盖和瓶两部分，浅覆盆式盖，束颈，圆肩，腹部扁圆形，向下渐收至底。盖上浮雕黄翡巧色龙钮，肩出对称双螭耳，腹部、肩部及底部边缘雕琢有绳纹。

134 清　冰糯种活环赏瓶 （一对）

长 78 毫米　宽 35 毫米　厚 21 毫米

◆ 冰糯种，质地细腻，飘绿。敞口，束颈、美人肩，圆腹，双圈
足，两侧双耳衔环，器型弧度优美。

135 清　冰种缠枝莲纹三狮衔环耳小赏瓶（一对）

高 125 毫米　腹径 54 毫米

♦ 冰种，质地细腻，色泽莹润，水绿色。器分盖口和瓶身两部分，直口，有唇，束颈、圆腹下收，圈足外撇。盖缘、瓶口及底足外沿均周饰回纹。盖上雕琢缠枝花卉纹，宝珠钮，衔三活环。颈部出三狮耳衔环，间饰蕉叶纹。腹部浅浮雕缠枝莲纹，为典型的清代宫廷玉雕代表作。

136 清　糯种春带彩竹叶钮蝴蝶牡丹耳赏瓶（一对）

高 140 毫米　宽 75 毫米　厚 33 毫米

◆ 糯种，质地细腻，色泽莹润，通体淡紫飘阳绿。椭圆形覆斗式盖，竹叶钮，平口，束颈，斜肩，肩出飘绿蝴蝶牡丹耳，耳下衔活环，扁圆腹，腹下收至底，圈足，足外撇。器身均双面雕工，一瓶浅浮雕两株麦穗和两只鹌鹑，另一瓶以同样工艺雕琢折枝竹叶，凤鸟栖息于枝头，一瑞兽呈伏卧状，昂首仰视。

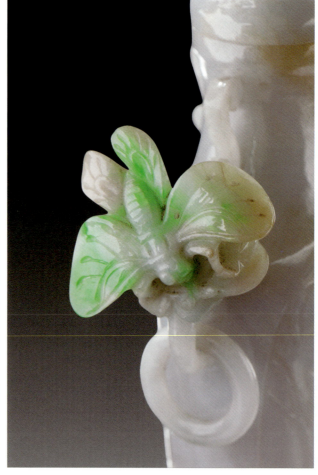

137 清　糯种阳绿乳钉纹连座筒瓶

高 310 毫米　直径 88 毫米

◆ 糯种，质地细腻，色泽莹润，带阳绿，局部带黄沁。以圆雕工艺雕琢呈筒式状，带盖，子母口，微束颈，溜肩，筒腹略敛，平底，连体带底座。此器盖各饰一圈星云纹和蕉叶纹，花状钮，器身满饰乳钉纹，排列致密。底座三弯腿带如意形足。

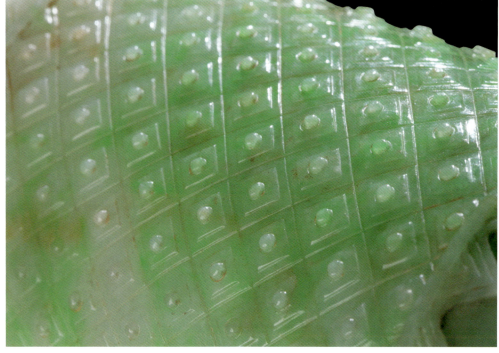

138 清　糯种三色瑞兽钮喜鹊登梅赏瓶

高 140 毫米　腹径 155 毫米

◆ 糯种，质地细腻，色泽莹润，黄、紫、绿三色，色彩丰富。覆盆式盖，盖顶双瑞兽钮，一坐一卧，昂头仰视，尾巴卷翘。圆口，平肩，腹下收至底。赏瓶周身以高浮雕和镂雕工艺雕琢梅枝及喜鹊，枝叶茂盛，梅花次第绽放。

139 清　糯种飘黄缠枝莲纹龙钮龙耳衔环大赏瓶

长 330 毫米　宽 145 毫米

◆　糯种，质地细腻，色泽莹润，水绿色，局部飘黄翡。方体盖，高浮雕龙钮，龙身卷曲，龙爪有力。方口沿、束颈、斜肩，肩出龙耳衔环，扁方腹，长方形足，足外撇。整器满工，浅浮雕缠枝莲纹和夔龙纹，盖两面有"乾隆御制"寄托款。

140 清 糯种红翡巧色松鼠葡萄大赏瓶

高 270 毫米　宽 260 毫米　厚 110 毫米

◆ 糯种，质地细腻，色泽莹润，水绿色。以镂雕、浮雕和掏膛工艺雕琢而成，中为赏瓶，分盖和瓶身两部分。覆钵式盖，瓶身呈扁圆状，平口，束颈，肩出镂雕夔龙纹耳，弧腹下收至底，实心足。赏瓶盖及腹部均饰以浅浮雕葡萄藤叶，藤蔓缠绕，间以红翡巧色松鼠、蜻蜓，螳螂，自然灵动。

赏瓶左右两侧圆雕甪端、天鸡各一。甪端呈站立状，微微抬首，双目圆睁，如意形鼻，张口露齿，双耳贴伏，独角后竖。天鸡栩栩如生，颇有气势。

141 清　冰糯种飘紫狮耳活环海棠炉

高 128.5 毫米　宽 131.9 毫米　厚 56.3 毫米

◆ 冰糯种，质地细腻，色泽莹润，淡紫色。整器作海棠状，盖钮
为四边各镂雕一狮耳衔环。口沿周饰回纹，炉身为双狮耳衔环，
底承三足，各雕琢有饕餮纹。

142 清　冰糯种仿痕都斯坦镂空熏炉

高 102.8 毫米　宽 130.6 毫米　厚 91.8 毫米

◆ 冰糯种，玉质细腻，色泽莹润，淡紫色。盖为帽状，盖钮为高
浮雕宝相花，盖身及盖沿环绕两圈镂空如意云头纹和缠枝莲纹。
炉身束颈圆腹，腹下内敛，下承外撇高圈足。炉身满雕花卉纹，
肩出两耳，耳浮雕西番莲纹衔环。这是晚清典型的仿痕都斯坦式
玉雕风格。

143 清　糯种阳绿狮钮活环三足炉

高 137 毫米　宽 108.7 毫米　厚 70 毫米

◆ 糯种，质地细腻，飘阳绿。覆钵式盖，盖顶平，高浮雕狮钮回首侧望，炉盖有四如意耳均匀分布，下衔活环。炉身为束颈，鼓腹、两侧饰对称镂雕双龙首衔环耳，炉底下承三兽足，兽首贴伏于炉身，足端雕成五趾兽爪状。

144 清　糯种红翡巧色双龙耳龙纹镂空熏炉

高 118 毫米　宽 156 毫米　腹径 114.3 毫米

◆ 糯种，玉质细腻，红翡巧色。分盖和炉身两部分，盖内外周饰回纹，云龙纹钮，红翡
巧色高浮雕双龙身。炉身满饰夔龙纹，肩两侧浮雕一对红翡巧色龙形立耳，双目圆睁，
双耳、双角后竖，足内卷，尾上翘卷曲。

145 清　冰种飘黄钵式炉

高 44 毫米　直径 122 毫米

◆ 冰种，质地细腻，晶莹通透，飘黄翡。
因炉形如钵而名，圆口，外撇，圈足。饱
满且规整，轮廓优美。

146 清　糯种飘黄钵式炉

直径 112 毫米　高 45 毫米

◆ 糯种，质地细腻，微带黄翡。因炉形如钵
而名，敞口束颈，鼓腹下收至底，厚圈足。造
型饱满且规整，轮廓优美。

◆ 糯种，质地细腻。覆碗式盖，盖两周弦纹，宝珠钮，钮上三侧各浮雕一夔龙。圆腹，腹部两周弦纹，束收圈底，肩出两只瑞兽耳衔环。三兽足，足外撇。

147 民国　糯种龙耳衔环三足炉

高 79 毫米　宽 185 毫米

◆ 糯种，质地细腻。覆碗式盖，盖两周弦纹，宝珠钮，钮上三侧各浮雕一夔龙。圆腹，腹部两周弦纹，束收圈底，肩出两只瑞兽耳衔环。三兽足，足外撇。

148 清　冰种阳绿星云纹龙耳衔环三足炉

高 145 毫米　宽 185 毫米

◆ 冰种，质地细腻，晶莹通透，飘阳绿，色彩艳丽。覆钵式盖，盖体高耸，满雕星云纹，
浮雕一螭龙为盖钮，龙做卷曲状，圆眼双睛，双耳后掠，嘴衔灵芝。炉身深束颈，广肩，
肩两侧以镂雕手法雕琢两个对称的龙首耳，耳下衔活环。龙圆眼凸出，翘鼻，双耳内卷，
嘴巴微张，气宇轩昂。

炉身雕琢饕餮纹，通饰星云纹，下承三兽面足，此炉用料极为上佳，琢工精良，为清代
中期宫廷玉雕的经典代表作。

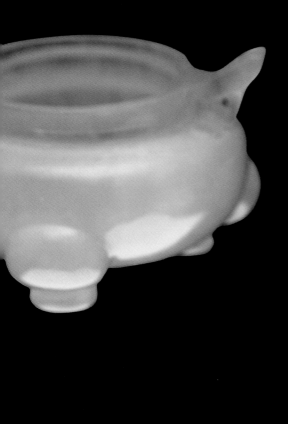

冰种，质地细腻，色泽莹润，覆钵式盖，龙钮，双目圆睁，两耳后竖，龙身卷曲。炉圆口，束颈，圆肩，肩出两耳，鼓腹，下承三足。

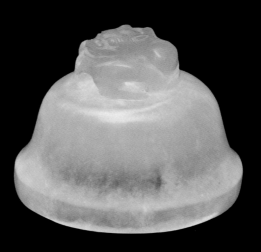

149 清　冰种龙钮三足炉

高 45 毫米　直径 49 毫米

◆ 冰种，质地细腻，色泽莹润，覆钵式盖，龙钮，双目圆睁，两耳后竖，龙身卷曲。炉圆口，束颈，圆肩，肩出两耳，鼓腹，下承三足。

150 清　糯种狮钮饕餮纹三足炉

高95毫米　宽52.5毫米　厚54.5毫米

◆ 糯种，温润细腻，深绿色。覆钵式盖，上高浮雕狮子，作侧身回首状，圆眼双睁，双耳后掠，瓶盖一圈饰瑞兽卷云纹。炉身弧形，满饰饕餮纹，有后配鎏金底座。

151 清　糯种喜鹊登梅镂空香熏（一对）

高 66.6 毫米　直径 33.3 毫米

◆ 糯种，色泽莹润，浅绿色。熏体呈筒形，上、下两部分，子母相扣，红木钮盖，直腹，带红木底座。腹部镂雕喜鹊登梅纹饰，梅枝粗壮有力，叶子自由舒展，梅花朵朵绽放，喜鹊或回首而望，或抬首仰望，嘴衔梅枝。

152 清　冰糯种狮钮双龙耳扁瓶

高 245 毫米　宽 130 毫米　厚 46 毫米

◆ 冰糯种，质地细腻，色泽莹润。覆斗式盖，盖顶平，高浮雕狮钮回首凝视，瓶方口、束颈、以镂雕工艺作夔龙纹耳，器身扁平，足外撇，正面有龙首衔环。

153 清　糯种饕餮纹飞龙耳炉

高 81 毫米　宽 165 毫米　腹径 128 毫米

◆ 糯种，温润细腻．缺盖。圆口，束颈，鼓腹，平底，圈足。口沿周饰回纹，肩两侧浅浮雕一对龙形立耳，龙首双目圆睁，嘴大张，双角后竖，双耳呈卷曲位于两侧，尾部卷曲翘起，炉腹部满饰云头如意纹和饕餮纹，炉盖遗失。

154 清　糯种飘阳绿龙钮双凤衔环耳三足炉

高 150 毫米　宽 180 毫米

◆　糯种，质地细腻，色泽莹润，飘阳绿。覆钵式盖，龙钮，双目圆睁，
两耳后竖，龙须向两侧卷翘，龙身蜷成一团，龙爪遒劲有力。炉圆口，
短颈，圆肩，肩出双凤耳衔环，鼓腹下收至底，器身光素，下承三足，
底刻"乾隆御制"寄托款。

155 清　冰种带绿绳结纹双龙衔环耳三足炉

高 125 毫米　宽 125 毫米

◆ 冰种，晶莹通透，质地细腻，带水绿。圆形盖，高浮雕三狮钮，一大狮子带两小狮子呈伏卧状，两小狮子相对而卧，中有一绣球附以飘逸缎带。器身圆口、溜肩、鼓腹，肩出双龙耳，耳下衔活环，腹部饰绳结纹，下承三足。此炉用料为木那种，用料极好。

高 125 毫米　宽 125 毫米

156 清　糯种阳绿五凤匜

长 170 毫米　宽 92 毫米　高 70 毫米

◆　糯种，质地细腻，飘阳绿，色彩艳丽。仿匜形，直口，方唇，腹壁近直，方底，口部一侧有流，另一侧夔龙纹耳，五只凤凰盘旋于口沿、器身，或回首而望，或展翅欲飞，或怡然休憩，口衔牡丹花卉、灵芝，阳绿巧色牡丹娇艳欲滴，凤凰形态各异，活灵活现，此匜用料上佳，工艺精湛，为典型清中期宫廷玉器。

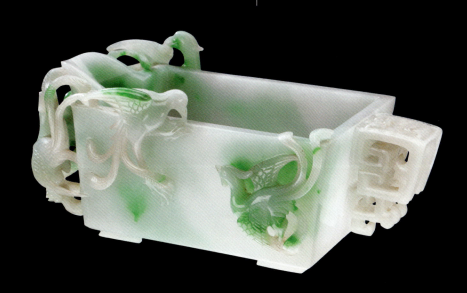

157 清　糯种飘紫饕餮纹夔龙耳觥

高 240 毫米　宽 180 毫米

◆　糯种，质地细腻，色泽莹润，通体淡紫色飘蓝花。
仿觥形。敞口，有唇，前有宽流，流上昂。镂雕夔龙
纹耳。器身分三段，上部以蕉叶纹作主饰，蕉叶下雕
回纹和寿字纹；腹部四面皆浅浮雕饕餮纹，下部饰蕉
叶纹，与上部遥相呼应。此觥为清代宫廷玉器仿古件。

高 240 毫米　宽 180 毫米

158 清　冰种饕餮纹出戟提梁卣

通高 270 毫米　宽 170 毫米

◆ 冰种，晶莹通透，淡绿色。仿青铜提梁卣形，盖上雕饰夔龙纹。器身分三段，圆口，收颈，溜肩，鼓腹，足外撇，外壁上下对称四出戟。上部浮雕夔龙纹；鼓腹四面皆饰饕餮纹；下部饰夔龙纹与上部相呼应。两侧镂雕龙纹，以活环与提梁相连。

159 清　糯种提梁活环花篮

通高 117 毫米　直径 61 毫米

◆ 糯种，玉质细腻，墨绿色。作花篮状，子母口，圈足，盖钮浮雕多个云头如意纹，盖一周浅浮雕缠枝花卉纹。两耳分别连活环各一，活环间连一提梁。篮体各竖四耳，耳下衔活环，腹部雕花卉纹，足下套活环，下挂彩穗。

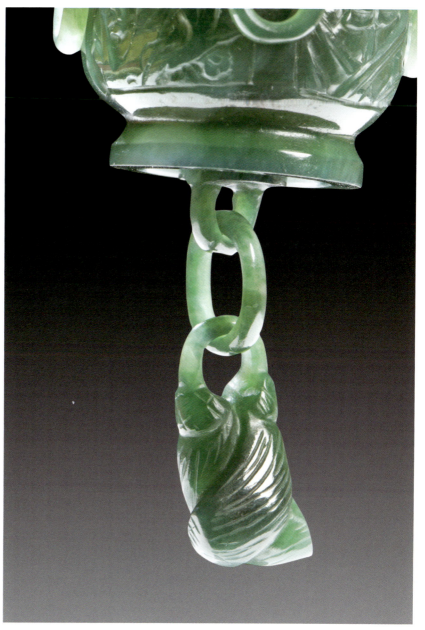